THE HAPPINESS BUG

Also by **Shelley Sykes**
Callum's Cure
Sexy Single & Ready to Mingle
Words of Inspiration
Hats to Heels
Forever Young
The Road to Wealth

Dr Edward de Bono
Has written 68 books
Just to name a few...
Six Thinking Hats
Lateral Thinking
How to be More Interesting
The Mechanism of the Mind
Tactics
The Happiness Purpose

The Happiness Bug

THE HAPPINESS BUG

How to CATCH the Happiness Bug & Bee Happy EVERY Day

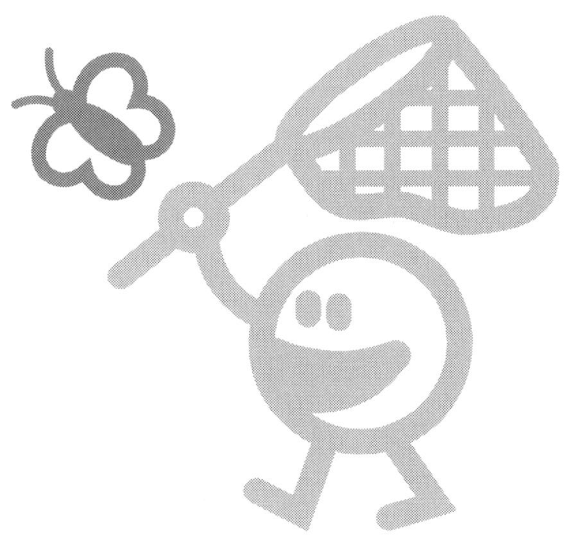

Shelley Sykes
WITH COMMENTARY BY
Edward De Bono

Sydney•New York•London•Vancouver•Hong Kong•Singapore•Deli•Cape Town

Beautiful Unlimited

A division of Beautiful Unlimited Inc

Sydney, NSW

Australia

For information about special discounts for bulk
purchases, please contact Beautiful Unlimited Special
Sales: +612 87650270
Or shelley@shelleysykes.com

Cover design by Coco Kochran
Typsetting by Bookhouse, Sydney
Distributed by Gary Allen in Australia and New Zealand
Printed and bound in Australia by Griffin Press

1 3 5 7 9 10 8 6 4 2

Library of Congress Cataloguing-in Publication Data is
available

ISBN 0–9775258–2–1

Self-Help/Family & Relationships/Psychology/Happiness

The Happiness Bug

Happiness is an attitude.

Thanks to all my special friends & family, who have
allowed me to develop my Happiness Attitude
And to Edward De Bono, my inspiration,
The author of the book 'Happiness Purpose'
Who made me realise I was 'normal' and
Nicknamed me
The Happiness Guru.

My mission is to inspire you to catch
The Happiness Bug for yourselves & share the
skills and tips to be happy each day.

As my son Callum Rory & his buddy WM Mitchell both
say:

"It isn't what happens to you in life that counts,
It's what you do about it that matters!"

Magic happens despite your circumstances.

Love and laughter always

Shelley x

Contents

Foreword by Edward de Bono

The pursuit of happiness and enjoyment is the legitimate purpose of life (as is recognised by the constitution of the United States of America). No one can be guaranteed happiness – and no one can demand that someone else supply him with it. But an individual has the right and the duty to pursue it in whichever form suits their talents and abilities.

A happy self is looked to as the basis of a happy society. A person who is not at ease with them selves is unlikely to be at ease with other people or society. Self-interest and self-importance are to be encouraged to the point of dignity; beyond that; they become counter-effective. The one proviso is; that it must not be obtained at the expense of others or at the expense of society. Shelley takes you to that happy place.

The Happiness Guru – Shelley Sykes supplies you with a net. Catch the Happiness bug and you can rediscover and highlight those talents and abilities, which can infect you for life.

A happy person is a fulfilled person. Catch **The Happiness Bug** and become fulfilled with the happiness you deserve.

Edward de Bono

Dr. Edward de Bono is regarded as the leading authority in the world in the direct teaching of thinking as a skill. He is the originator of lateral thinking, which puts idea creativity on a logical basis for the first time in history. He has written 68 books with translations into 39 languages. His work is in use in thousands of schools around the world. His Six Hat frame for parallel thinking is used equally by top economists and by more primitive societies in the highlands of Papua New Guinea. His instruction in thinking has been sought by many of the world's largest corporations such as IBM, Shell, and Nokia etc.

A personal friend and mentor to Shelley . . . he nicknamed her 'The Happiness Guru'

www.edwarddebono.com
www.edwdebono.com
www.debono.org

The Beginning

by the author,
Shelley Sykes

Why you and why now?

If you are ready for a lot more happiness, energy, love and laughter in your life, then this is the book for YOU.

The psychologists of today state that for many people it takes the first 40 years to get over the first 5! This may be true for me too, but as a small child I must have experienced a lot of happiness in my early days, but then like most teenagers it seemed to vanish throughout my teens and early adulthood only popping up spasmodically. I just couldn't seem to 'get back' that feeling of happiness on a regular basis. Then the '**If only's**' set in. If only, I got into that school, if only I achieved 'A' grades, if only I got that degree, job, dress, man, car, income then I would be happy! Happiness would be mine once again! I seriously searched and tried hard to change myself and control my life in order to get back into that happy carefree state, but it was an up hill struggle being young, with so many restrictions and lack of resources, or so I told myself, circumstances never seemed to be 'just right'.

I really wanted the **Happiness Experience** back, the feeling of 'being happy' with it's great, cosy, safe, uplifting, energising and yes addictive ways. You feel great when you are happy, not a care in the world. **Unfortunately, like a thief in the night 'something' or 'someone' happens to you and you're back into that rotten place called 'Ok-ness' or if worse; anger, depression, lethargy and/or frustration.**

Spookily most humans are in these states most days, but not for much longer, because I found **the secret to be happy every day despite life's circumstances** and that is what I am going to share with you in this book.

Siimon Reynolds the Australian Advertising Genius, says people are like magnets they are attracted to you at the right time and place whether it is to teach a lesson or to learn one.

It wasn't until I became magnetised to the Mr Lateral Thinking Mastermind, Dr Edward De Bono, who having read my inspirational book *'Callum's Cure'* nicknamed me **'The Happiness Guru.'**

Why was I a Happiness Guru? Didn't you have to be old to be a 'Guru'? Edward went on to explain that a 'Guru' is someone, who has the wisdom of experience and has the heart and desire to inspire others with those experiences in order to enlighten anyone ready to listen. The audience are normally people travelling on the same path – so happily that could be you!

Edward had written the book the *'Happiness Purpose'* back in 1979, which explained the value of happiness and how in an ideal world people should and could behave even in adverse conditions in order to stay happy. He suggested I read it, so that I would understand more clearly why he called me 'The Happiness Guru'.

Getting hold of a copy of the *Happiness Purpose* book was the first challenge!

It had gone out of print several years ago, since Edward has written another 65 books since, but as the universe had it, my friend Tad from the National Speakers Association suggested we might find it in the library of the Australian Institute of Management. We were lucky.

I was blown over, when I read his book – I had such affinity with Edward's words of wisdom. It was as if Edward had written a book about my actions and reactions, yet he wrote this book when I was just a young girl. I saw myself nod in agreement to each page. **Tears of joy ran down my face as the realisation dawned on me that, being in a 'happy state' was 'normal' and certainly far healthier.**

"If only I had read this book years ago"

… I extolled to Edward, "I would not have worried about being different to other people and I could have enjoyed being me, as I do now far sooner!"

There were so many tips and tools in his book that I had only just learnt. **I could have caught the Happiness Bug so much earlier.** Edward just smiled with his knowing smile and said "Shelley you wouldn't be you, if you hadn't gone through the experiences that you did."

Everything is just perfect – for all of us.

Throughout the centuries, we have all learnt through our predecessors-experiences and their mistakes. I do believe you don't have to experience everything and do the hard yards to learn the lessons. If we did, we wouldn't be able to progress as quickly, if at all. As the old adage says "why re-invent the wheel?" **I certainly want to make your life's journey to happiness so much easier** and less bumpy than my own. Perhaps that is what makes a Guru a great teacher. They have made more mistakes than most and then teach others the smartest, quickest way, for the best results. Yet was I 'ready' to be a Guru?

You may already gather that I am quite a confident lady, yet integrity is one of my main values in life and I was still not comfortable or sure if I qualified to be a 'Guru'. After phoning around a few of my very close friends in different parts of the globe and informing them of Edward's new name for me, I asked them if they could visualise their friend 'Shelley Sykes' as 'The Happiness Guru' too? Their response was unanimous. United gasps of "that's soo you" or "Oh yes", "absolutely darling, you're always Miss Happy". These were my friends, who had known me for years through thick and thin. It was all the endorsement I needed to comfortably place 'The Happiness Guru hat' on my head. I was already passionately supporting people with their health, wealth, image, relationships and self-esteem it seemed now only natural to place it under the 'Happiness brolly'.

Health, Wealth and Happiness! It's the name I chose for a TV show I have written and directed and I was so thrilled, when I received an email from Siimon Reynolds saying "you certainly live up to your name "The Happiness Guru" – after interviewing him for the show. It was our very first meeting, which was a wonderful calamity in itself and only lasted 10 minutes. I laughed with joy, because most people would have shrivelled and dug a hole with embarrassment if they had seen what went on that day! The whole interview had been something out of a comedy skit. I felt like a Goldie Horn or a female John Cleese from Faulty Towers, rolled in to one!

My film crew had not been able to make the shoot, so had given me quick lessons in lighting and camera . . . The appointment had changed both in time and date and then been rescheduled and some how I had a time 30 minutes later than I was expected. Arriving late was not a great start.

It took me 20 minutes to set up the lights, the camera on the tripod, whose one leg just kept dropping . . . Siimon walked in announcing calmly that he had only 10 minutes left for the interview before his next appointment.

I optimistically claimed 'I was ready' as the tripod slipped once again and stated 'that we would be one-take wonders!' as I tightened the tripod leg once again.

The camera was rolling, the lights were bright, the flowers on the desk were positioned in the right place in front of Siimon, I just had to run around the desk and switch from crew to presenter . . . I informed Siimon what I was going to ask him and suggested the kind of answer that would be ideal . . . we began.

The first question and the first answer, both were smooth . . . I excused myself, ran around the table and re ran the movie to check for sound, light and picture quality. Bummer! The lights were casting a shadow. I switched the lights off and ran round the desk.

Action! Question one again, two, three and four! It was a wrap and we finished at the stroke of 11 am – both professionals, both with integrity, both coming from the heart.

I managed to take a few cut-aways as I was leaving the office, Siimon already deep in conversation in his next meeting.

I giggled at the horror my crew or any 'serious' TV or film production team would express, at the whole fiasco – yet I had a great piece of footage from one of Australia's busy millionaires. He too must have enjoyed the humour and fun of it all. It certainly was high energy.
Laugh, you had to or you would cry!

After wearing 'The Happiness Guru' hat for awhile and being in the flow, **I realised it would be a pleasure, not a duty to pass on this amazing secret to Happiness, which has been so elusive to me in the past.**

I am sure you will be delighted to catch the most contagious bug in the world and never want to get rid of it! But remember the choice is yours. For the sceptics, I suggest you try it and see.

With the genius resource of **Edward De Bono** the creator of lateral thinking by my side, **offering to let me use extracts from his *Happiness Purpose* book** in order for you to benefit from his amazing insights, we have found a sure way for you all to catch **the Happiness Bug**.

Like all bugs some find it much easier and quicker to catch than others. Unlike most conventional bugs those of you, who are the most healthy tend to catch it easily, but those of you with a heavy load, toughened by life, first need to unload your baggage, soften up and take a long earned break before the bug sets to work and I'll explain HOW in the following chapters.

Einstein said that 'success comes to those that are persistent in finding new ways, when the old ones don't work.' Be persistent now and read this book and let the **Happiness Experience** begin. It is time for you to shine your light, be happy and then make a positive difference to the world and contaminate others around you!

Here's to the best disease ever created for a happy you and a happier world!

Shelley Sykes BSc MBA Dip Psych Dip Journo
The Happiness Guru
Speaker, Author, TV & Radio Presenter

www.shelleysykes.com

chapter 1

What is the 'Happiness Syndrome'?

 **TIP**

Happiness is an attitude. Magic happens despite our circumstances

**SHELLEY SYKES
THE HAPPINESS GURU**

Luckily I realised that I had caught **the Happiness Bug** (several years ago). It was quite by accident and I haven't been able to shake it off since. The weird thing is my life has been far from perfect. For quite a while I was mystified, firstly that I could feel happy under some of the most trying circumstances and even more mystified that I was being ridiculed for having this **Happiness Syndrome**! I was teased for being a 'Poly Anna', everything in the garden is alright type, ostracised by some for being an ostrich burying my head in the sand and not facing up to 'reality'. I felt I was in a no-win situation. As Bart Simpson in the cartoon 'The Simpson's' says, "You're damned if you do (feel happy) and damned if you don't!" I felt very 'odd' and different for feeling happy most of the time.

At the start of my working career when I worked for IBM I was trained at the Dale Carnegie Business School in South Africa. Dale, long since dead, was purported to be the best sales man in the world in his day and his techniques are still being used now, because his focus was all about people. He wrote the best-selling book *'How to win friends and influence people'*. This is what he said about happiness:

'Happiness doesn't depend upon 'who you are' or 'what you have'; it depends solely upon 'what you think.'
Dale Carnegie

Edward De Bono, a genius of our time and famous for his 'lateral thinking' phenomena and author of *'The Six Thinking Hats'* echoes the same message. He nicknamed me **The Happiness Guru,** because of my ability to think creatively.

In this book I will prove these mastermind statements to be true and lead by example, showing you how YOU TOO can re-think your life by catching **The Happiness Bug** and enjoy life's benefits with **The Happiness Experience.**

The Happiness Syndrome is a condition that no matter what happens to you in life, you can still see the positive in any situation. You still feel good even if shit happens in your life. We all know it does, whether you're rich, poor, fat, thin, black or white, gay or straight, living in Argentina or living in Zimbabwe or anywhere in between for that matter.

Life has its challenges. It is just part of our living experience. What is great about the **Happiness**

Syndrome is it is consistent and no one ever loses. Everyone can catch it from small children to very old people, **it's free** and it is very uplifting, humbling, attractive to others and very contagious.

We've all seen a person walking down the street smiling and we have instinctively smiled back. That's the **Happiness Syndrome** at work. Most of us have at one stage or another heard some one laugh and laugh – we don't know what at, but then we start to giggle too. That is the **Happiness Syndrome!** You just can't help yourself in the end and why would you? It feels GREAT!

The Happiness Syndrome allows you to feel joy, despite your circumstances.

I must be honest and say that I, the Happiness Guru wasn't always happy. Sometimes you have to feel the pain to appreciate the joys.

We all have our own stories that have moulded us into the people we are today.

Nothing is ever wrong.
Everything is perfect.

Perhaps those stories lead us to new belief systems that worked for us in the past, but in the present and future these stories can work against us.

Let me use my stories as examples and answer some of the questions we, as humans, pose to ourselves and some of the statements we perhaps have been living with from childhood that have kept us from **'shining our light'**.

As the stories unfold I pose questions for you to think about in relation to yourself and your life. Hopefully, when seen through the eyes and experiences of another you will get an "ah ah" or two. These are realisations that before perhaps weren't apparent, but that 'knowing' now will make your life easier.

At the end of the day **'we' are the most important people in our own lives**. It is our duty to ensure we survive and in my opinion if we can survive happily then our journey will be much more pleasant.

L Ron Hubbard was a big time movie screenwriter in Hollywood working with some of the top stars such Errol Flynn. His films were massive financial hits. He was an extremely wealthy man and a philanthropist. He wanted to be MAD, as I call it (to **Make A D**ifference to peoples lives). After years of studies he came to the conclusion that **our primary function on this planet is to survive happily. It is the degree to which we survive that determines how happy we become.** Our skill at communication with one another was key. From countless tests he and his researchers discovered that our state of mind and the way it stores everything going on in our environments can greatly effect our actions. His discovery lead to the system he calls 'Dianetics', which means through the mind. He created a program that helps people clear some of the negative data stored in our 'reactive mind' area. This is memory often stored when unconscious, traumatised or in a weakened state, even at birth and rears itself when we experience a similar situation.

Hubbard was so amazed at the power of our mind and it's capacity to store 'everything' we hear, smell see and for that matter, don't need to see, but can still sense. He was able to demonstrate how people in operating theatres or car accidents that are in a state of unconsciousness are still picking up messages from the surgeons or ambulance people and react to their statements in life without understanding why. For example, one man heard the ambulance-man ask the other 'how was his girl friend and how they were getting along?' His response was 'she got too clingy' and he 'needed his freedom'. "It was time to move on." Simple statements between two work-colleagues. It was raining, the ambulance siren was blurting out as they were driving to the hospital and this whole scene had been recorded in the injured man's subconscious.

Years later the injured man Peter, had met the woman of his dreams, happy and in love one evening he picked her up in his car to take her to his parents for dinner. It was raining. An ambulance drove past with it's siren going and out of the blue Peter got the 'feeling' that his girl was **'too clingy'** and **'that he needed his freedom'**. He stopped the car and told her **it was time to move on**...

Now this 'self-sabotage' happens a lot. A lady in hospital hears she will never get better and it is almost a 'self fulfilling prophesy' even if it was not directed to the person that heard the comment – that lady never got better, to the surprise of all. It is scary that this is possible. That we can react to things that we heard out of context and that can be holding us back or stopping us follow our paths to happiness.

Often we have no idea where it is coming from and why we do these things. Peter didn't have a clue. One minute he had found his true love and the next he was lonely and had blown it with the best thing in his life. He only found out after being counselled in Dianetics. Luckily for him he managed to 'clear' this reaction and get back with his girl.

I am a great believer that any religion is good if the believer feels happy and well, motivated and inspired to do good for themselves and others as a result of their beliefs. The Scientologists of the world follow L. Ron Hubbard's philosophies for personal healing and growth using such tools as Dianetics. I had presumed wrongly that Scientology was just a religion, but it is more than that. Like many religions, it is a way of being and thinking.

As we know a lot of the movie stars today such as John Travolta and Tom Cruise are followers of L. Ron Hubbard's teachings or are commonly called Scientologists. In fact, it hit the news this week that Tom and his expectant partner Katie have planned to have a 'silent birth' for their first child so that their baby will not pick up on any negative 'words' or sounds of angst.

It now makes sense to me. You don't want your baby coming into the world hearing violent screams or terrible noises that can upset them in their future. I just feel relieved I was laughing and joking when my little man was born (I had a planned caesarean so didn't feel a thing . . . but then what was said when I wasn't around? He has cerebral palsy!

TIP

I personally don't subscribe to any one particular system.
I find a way to get the most positive result in the best way
available.

SHELLEY SYKES
THE HAPPINESS GURU

For the purpose of this book we are going to apply the more practical tools that can be applied by most people, but if you have serious illnesses or have been traumatised and it still haunts you then Dianetics is definitely worth trying out first, during or after my tools and techniques for applied happiness, so that you can have the greatest benefits.

We all do react differently to similar events, often due to our **personalities, experiences** and **states** at the time. A child when tired is far more irrational than a child that is full of energy – this is true for me still. I can be as calm and cool about many situations, but if I am extremely tired then I can burst into tears at the slightest criticism or confrontation.

We are humans not robots.
It is what makes us 'loveable'.

The **Happiness Syndrome** does not get 'rid' of all irrational behaviour, but it does allow you to be more kind to yourself when you are 'feeling irrational'. In my tired state I just take myself off to bed or excuse my behaviour gently for being tired. I remind myself 'tomorrow is another day'. It also allows you to 'switch back' in an instant to a 'happy state' by focusing on what is great about the situation, your life right now. It is very exciting to be able to choose to be happy, whenever you want.

If you want to be able to feel happy most of the time, enjoy your journey, relax and have more friends, more energy, feel healthier and laugh more then let your **Happiness Experience** begin!

Like all stories it is better to start at the beginning. We really need to get to know ourselves and what makes us tick the way we do and ultimately what makes us happy.

United Kingdom – the first years

Life's not fair

At 5 years old I remember realising life wasn't fair, when my favourite Barbie doll and favourite basket were taken from me in anger and thrust on to the steps of a cinema in the city for some other lucky child, because I had been naughty, annoying or something – perhaps mum was just tired and stressed and just over-reacted. I was horrified and disgusted. My happiness bubble seemed to start shrinking from that day. Remember there is no right or wrongs. No one is to blame. It just is.

A belief system created at 5 years old was 'good things come, but can easily be taken away'. This belief expressed it's self over and over again throughout my life. Made money, lost money. Got a great guy, lost a great guy…until **The**

Happiness Bug struck. The old belief had to be replaced if I wanted to have new outcomes.

After being zapped by **The Happiness Bug**, the new belief system became and still is:

 **TIP**

'Nice things/people come and may go. They will always be replaced with even nicer things/people. There is always a time and place for everything and everyone. All is well.'

SHELLEY SYKES
THE HAPPINESS GURU

When did you first realise life wasn't fair?
How can that be turned around to be an advantage for you?

Self-reliant or needy?

I think my first worries came when I was 7 years old and was thrown through the rear side car window, after grabbing my younger sister who, had moments before sat next to me in the back, but was now flying through the air head first heading towards the front windscreen. I had grabbed her dress and with the car careening over the road out of control she fell back on top of me just in time, as the car smashed abruptly into a solid Yorkshire dry stonewall. The impact of the crash and the weight of my baby sister struck me so hard my head went crashing through the thickened glass and the next thing I knew, I was being carried into the ambulance with my mum by my side gazing down at me, her face streaked with blood and tears rolling down her cheeks. I was horrified that my mummy was hurt and I wanted to reach out and hug her better, but I couldn't. I couldn't move. I felt impotent, vulnerable and small. Fear overwhelmed me that I could lose those dearest to me. My happiness bubble was shrinking.

Fear of loss made me toughen up. I had to become more independent and more self-reliant just in case. This manifested its self by keeping myself distant from other people so that I wouldn't get hurt and by becoming **too** self-reliant.

 **TIP**

The happiness syndrome resulted in the belief change that 'it is alright to ask for help and it is ok to be vulnerable at times.'
SHELLEY SYKES
THE HAPPINESS GURU

When did you first realise that you had to become self-reliant or needy?
What can you do differently to bring back balance?

Being different

At 8 years old I never wanted to go back to school. I was constantly teased by my classmates; for having different coloured eyes, but by 8 the teasing had become vicious and I felt I didn't have a friend in the world.

That was until my creative loving mum told me I was "**An Egyptian Princess**" and my eyes were proof. Only Egyptian Princesses had special eyes – one blue and one brown! I wanted to be just like everyone else, but I knew I was different. My difference became my saviour, because thrilled that there was a wonderful reason to my difference, I proudly went to school the next day and passionately told everyone that I was 'royalty'. I soon attracted a girlie gang!

My difference attracted many, but my difference attracted disdain and envy too. I wanted to be liked by **'everyone'**. Instead of focusing on the friends I attracted I worried about those that became mean, until the happiness syndrome kicked in.

The new belief,

TIP

'We are all unique and special. Love the ones that love you. We can't please everyone. It just is.'

SHELLEY SYKES
THE HAPPINESS GURU

What is your difference?
Do you have a positive story? It's ok to make one up that suits your personality.

Am I enough?

At 10 years old I decided I wanted to become a doctor inspired by Marie Curie the 18th century physicist, who discovered Radium. She had made such a difference to people's lives with X-rays and medicine in general. I wanted to make a difference like her too. So I really needed to pass the exams to get into grammar school. I really, really wanted to get there and I prayed and crossed my fingers after sitting the entrance exam. I realised I needed all the help I could get after being told I wasn't the brightest of kids (which I believed to be the 'truth'). Luckily my exam results were borderline and I just scraped in.

The joy and exuberation on receiving the letter of acceptance to the Brighouse Girls Grammar School was immense for about half an hour, until I heard the whispered bickering comments about the cost of the uniforms! Parents...couldn't they ever be happy for you?

The six weeks school holidays couldn't go fast enough. I was happy that my first day of Grammar school arrived. I loved my new school uniform and blazer (that were 3 times too big – my parents were determined I would get good use of it). It had taken me hours of practice to learn how to tie my tie. I felt so grown up.

This was definitely a new beginning and I was filled with expectation. I set off to school happily like a mule laden with all my books, bags, sports kit, and tennis-racket. My happy disposition popped like a chewing gum bubble all over my face, when the other kids in the class laughed at me when they saw me hot with exertion, weighed down with everything, wearing a uniform for third year students. Why were they laughing? Where were their things? I was horrified and blushed furiously – I stood out like a sore thumb.

It didn't take long before they noticed my eyes and laughed and teased even more when I told them I was a 'princess'. Why wasn't my uniqueness working here? The salt was rubbed into my wounds even more when the teacher asked if I had left home pointing at all my bags and told me we didn't get lockers in the first term. The class laughed once again. I was so embarrassed. This was not a good start. I had nobody to turn to for moral support either. My primary school friends were in different classes and I didn't have any allies.

By recess, girls had already gathered into gangs and I was standing all alone a 'geek', no longer a 'princess with her followers', on the netball courts when a group of giant girls approached me. Two of them pinned down my arms as the others pushed me forward. The cackles and laughs from these witches were deafening as they shoved me closer to the goal posts. My classmates were wide eyed and didn't make a move to help and the big girls looked back menacingly at the on lookers and yet laughed mischievously amongst them-selves. Suddenly the top of the goal post dropped scarily close to my nose and I thought they were going to try and shove my head through the hoop, but then my beautiful new tie was yanked and the realisation that they were trying to hang me filled me with absolute disbelief.

I cried out and fought to get free, but these monsters were strong. Suddenly the goal post was pushed back up and I was forced onto my tiptoes just as the bell rang to announce that recess was over.

Everyone just left, all making their way back to their classrooms, leaving me hanging tied to the tilted netball post!

The knots on my tie around the post and my neck were so tight that I thought I would faint. How could this be happening to me? This was supposed to be a 'good' school. None of the teachers had noticed I was missing.

It was a beautiful September day and the sun was shining on the orange tints of the autumn leaves, but it was very chilly. My hands were red and numb with cold. I had to wait 10 minutes before the caretaker came to my rescue. "It was a school tradition" he mumbled – "happened every year to some poor new First Year."

On returning to my class, I was told off by the teacher for being late!

Life was so unfair!

By the end of the first week, it was announced by my class teacher to all the class that I had the lowest grades in the class – the dumb one. It appeared that the cooler and smarter you were in this school, the more friends you attracted. I just was not cool or smart enough – YET.

 **TIP**

It isn't what happens to you in life that counts, it's what you do about it that matters. Magic happens despite your circumstances.

SHELLEY SYKES
THE HAPPINESS GURU

Damned if you do and damned if you don't

At school I was scorned and ignored for not being smart enough. Even the class bullies and naughty girls were smarter than me initially. I hated not being enough and so I decided to do what ever it took to be the smartest and best in the class. I spent most break times in the library reading, every lunchtime doing my homework and I even read books at the bus stops on the way to and from school. I would spend every night reading, even by torchlight until late in the night, trying to understand 'what on earth' the teachers were trying to teach me, often crying with exasperation. Nothing seemed to come easy and worse there was no one at home that could help me. Mum was a bank manager and more commercially trained and dad studied art at university and their passion was property styling.

At home I was scorned for being a 'swot'. My sister disowned me. I was an embarrassment to her walking around with my head in a book! Missy Goodie-two-shoes! She became the rebel. My parents, sociable, out-going, party people found my withdrawn, serious, studious new persona odd and unnatural. They worried that I was pushing myself too hard and aiming too high for my capabilities. Perhaps a physiotherapist would be more practical than aiming to be a doctor. I was shocked that my parents weren't supportive. Weren't they, as parents, supposed to be encouraging me to work harder?
Dammed if you do and dammed if you don't!

I didn't seem to fit anywhere. I was damned for not being smart enough by my peers at school and I was damned at home for being too studious and suppressing my social bubbly personality at home.

The fire of desire to be liked and belong was ignited and I was determined to 'show them all!'

My belief back then was **I was not enough.** To get on and be liked you had to be smart and not stand out too much. I became withdrawn, studied night and day and by the third year, won best class prize and achieved top placement in maths. Even the teachers liked you when you were smart. The difference in **attitude** was amazing and I knew then, which one I preferred.

TIP

*After catching **The Happiness Bug** I realised that we are all enough and we can all achieve our dreams if we desire it enough and take action. Yet we must do it for ourselves and not to please others or be accepted by them.*

SHELLEY SYKES
THE HAPPINESS GURU

What made you feel 'not enough'?
What did you do to empower yourself?

TIP

You can't please everyone.
Dreams and desires if strong enough will be realised
With action and persistence.

SHELLEY SYKES
THE HAPPINESS GURU

What was your dilemma?
What can you be proud of for overcoming?

On my own

I managed to get through high school with only a few hiccups after that. I really loved it. I loved the variety of the subjects and the encouragement of the teachers (once I had improved), I was on every school sports team, in the choir, drama club and became House School Captain in the 6th form (Year 12). I made some very special school friends – all bright and all naturally very smart. I felt privileged to be amongst them.

Unfortunately, my **insecurities** of **not being enough** always surfaced at exam time. My confidence in my ability would fly through the window and I would focus on the possibility of failure. I would shake with anxiousness and often would miss-read the questions, because I was so nervous. Despite all the studying and encouragement from teachers I still had my doubts. **Of course whatever we focus on becomes our reality** and so my exam results would never be as great at they could or should have been.

At 17 years old I didn't get high enough grades, 3 A's to be accepted into university to study medicine. So, still determined, I decided to resit them the following year.
My parents had had enough. They were exasperated that I just wouldn't accept the results, forget the dream of being a doctor and just accept the university placement for pharmacy or go out and get a job!

How could they ask me to give up my dream? There was no way. **Didn't all the psychologists and experts say dream big and never quit?** I refused to quit and defied my parents by leaving home to go to a college that focused on helping students revise, relax and resit their exams with deft.

I realised I was on my own and had to take responsibility for myself.

TIP

Persistence is one of the keys to achieving success.

SHELLEY SYKES
THE HAPPINESS GURU

When did you first realise you were on your own?
What did you do to get yourself closer to your dreams?

Why me?

I worked so hard at college and struggled to live on my own that year. By the time the exams came I was feeling confident until the night before when my current boyfriend finished with me. I became a wreck and lost my focus.

I didn't apply all the training I had had. I didn't trust my own gut and I didn't believe in myself enough. I was allowing others to dictate whether I would succeed or not. Needless to say I didn't get the results I needed.

"My life was ruined! All that hard work for nothing! My parents were right all along my boyfriend is a jerk and I'm just not smart enough!"

I allowed myself to use the excuses and wallow in self-pity. I returned home and **gave up my control to others**, this time to my parents. I dutifully got a job.

TIP

One cardinal sin that thwarts 'being happy' is to give up your control to others and quit your dreams! Remember to never quit and stay true to YOU.

SHELLEY SYKES
THE HAPPINESS GURU

What I didn't realise at the time is there are no right and wrongs in life. It just is and all the trials and set backs were amazing lessons that brought forth my light and uniqueness.

TIP

How do you know what you like and don't like unless you try things out and experience pleasure or pain? Life is a journey of lessons and they become easier when you allow yourself to just be and experience them.

SHELLEY SYKES
THE HAPPINESS GURU

What I did find was that every time I 'resisted' the lessons of life they would be thrown back at me over and over again until I would learn the lessons.

Life's not fair

Life's not fair. So what!

Self-reliant or needy?

Who cares just ask for help when you need it

Being Different

Being different means I can help in my own unique way!

Am I enough?

Yes, I am enough for right now.

Damned if you do, damned if you don't

So what if I can't please everyone – I will do what makes me happy and enjoy the journey touching those few on the way!

On my own

I am not alone. We are all part of this amazing universe.

Why me?

Why NOT me? Life is never boring; it's quite an adventure.

You know that you have the **Happiness Syndrome** when you ask yourself the questions I listed above and laugh. If you can enjoy the answers to the questions above, because the negative emotions have been replaced, then you will enjoy the **Happiness Experience** that results from it.

Life has a unique way of bringing on the lessons, the teacher or the opportunities whether you are ready or not.

What I have learnt is that if we embrace all that appears on our life's journey we can actually have a great fun filled adventure when we wear 'rose coloured glasses' instead of the bleak black goggles or easier still catch **The Happiness Bug**. In order to see through rose coloured lenses we first have to relax and enjoy **'being who we are, just as we are'**.
Our first priority is to honour ourselves and congratulate the fact we got here safely so far. We have to like ourselves.

In the past 'to love and like yourself' was taboo with many of the controlling religious fractions and people in general and still may be in your family. To like you and put yourself first was nicknamed 'conceit', 'vanity', and 'selfish'.

The **Happiness Syndrome** defies this belief and says **'who are we not to love ourselves first and shine our light'** so that we can too pass on the love and respect to others **like a ripple effect**. Nelson Mandela used this line in his inaugural speech as President.

Our personal power is in our ability to like ourselves. The more we like and respect ourselves the more energy we radiate and more easily attract success in health, wealth and happiness into our lives.

It is hard to explain, only now the Quantum Physicians are only just agreeing with what the spiritual leaders have been saying for centuries – the power lies within us and we create our own realities.

 **TIP**

To be happy we have to think differently about ourselves and appreciate how wonderful we are. We are miracles in our own right and as such deserve respect and love from ourselves first. Spookily the more we love ourselves the more we attract the love of others.

**SHELLEY SYKES
THE HAPPINESS GURU**

Dr John Demartini is known for his chiropractic work and his philosophies that LIFE IS ALL ABOUT BALANCE. Happiness or gratitude comes after feeling the pain or loss; it's the Ying and Yang, the positive and negative, the male and female, black and white. Like many of us he states that as humans we all have 7 value areas in life which are: Social, Health, Friends and Family, Career, Spiritual, Finances and Relationships and it is in our best interests if we wish to be successful and improve our self-esteem that we gain balance in all the seven areas. If we are out of balance in one area, it has an effect on all the other areas of our lives.

When I met John I was pretty strong in 5 value areas but my love relationships were low (I wasn't in a loving romantic relationship) and my finances were negative!
By looking at my seven areas of life I knew then that I had to focus on strengthening those two areas. Did this mean that I was unhappy? No, I was still happy I stayed focused on what was right with my relationships and what was right

with finance – grateful for the lessons that had made me smarter and appreciative.

Is balancing life simple? No, it is a constant effort, which makes life more adventurous!

John Demartini left home at 13 years old and lived on the streets of California, because he had a wish to surf and had already been labelled 'un-academic'. He couldn't read or write properly, because of dyslexia – now a voracious reader and acclaimed academic over coming obstacles, he has defied the odds proving that magic and miracles do work despite our circumstances.

He overcame his perceived weaknesses and his mission is to touch people to break through their negative beliefs to live their best lives. He wants to be, what I call being 'madder' and 'Make A Difference' globally. Nelson Mandela, Tony Robbins, Andrew Mathews, Madonna, Brian Tracy, Oprah, Bono, Roger Hamilton, Richard Branson, L Ron Hubbard, Edward De Bono and myself, Shelley Sykes – The Happiness Guru to name just a few, **all have a similar desire to make a BIG difference so that we can all achieve our dreams and live a more abundant happier life in love and unity.** Its possible!

Have they all got **The Happiness Bug** and suffering from the **Happiness Syndrome**?
Yes absolutely. We are all sending out our ripples to touch the lives of people around us.

You can join our ranks!

I think you will gather that the solution to **Happiness** is not about controlling life. Does shit still happen to Oprah, Richard Branson, Madonna or Bono . . . yes it does, but the secret to having **The Happiness Bug** is **how** you handle the shit and **how** you 'see' that shit, whether it is another interesting lesson on life's journey or not.

 **TIP**

Magic happens despite our circumstances. It isn't what happens to you in life that counts, its what you do about it that matters.

SHELLEY SYKES
THE HAPPINESS GURU

In the next chapters I will give you cool ways to learn the skills of catching and keeping **The Happiness Bug** even in the trying times so that it no longer becomes an effort.

Instead it is who you are that is important, a happy person with dignity, with a healthy, successful outlook on life, a person that people can admire.

We all get doubts, but I urge you now to only focus on what you feel is fabulous about yourself!

Where are you in your list of values?
What 10 things are you good at?
What can you be proud of?
How have you made a difference to others so far?
What do your friends and family like about you?
What are some of your happy memories?

What do you like doing that brings a smile to your face and energy to continue?
What is your biggest dream?
How can you be MAD (Make a difference) or be madder?

Make a **list of all your good traits** and write them on a piece of paper and use it as a bookmark and read your list daily!

Tiger Woods, the number 1 worlds best golfer, never focuses on his weak strokes only on the strong ones so that he never has to revert to his weak strokes and that is what we are going to do. **Focus on all our strengths** and build on those.

Edward de Bono's comments

Dignity and happiness are the twin aims for **The Happiness Bug**. Happiness is based on peace and enjoyment. Dignity is based on self-worth and on a person 'filling their skin'. A person has dignity when they are happy with themselves – not because others have suggested that they should be, but because a person is.

The self is very important. Self-care has priority of consideration over all other cares – but not necessarily priority in a conflict of interests. There is to be balance between extremes. There is to be balance in attention paid to different things, in a mix which has different ingredients, between the inner world and the outer world, between adjusting to the circumstances or changing them, between activity and awareness.

People are to enjoy, value and respect themselves.

Respect is a quiet acknowledgement of the existence and the rights of oneself, of others and of society. **Respect is to be the foundation upon which happiness can be built.** Respect is vision that is both clear and positive. Dignity is regarded as a better protection against selfishness than self-denial.

Dignity is the point at which self-love is the same as happiness.

chapter 2

One door closes, another opens

 **TIP**

Nothing is ever wrong, there are always opportunities often bigger and better than the last!

**SHELLEY SYKES
THE HAPPINESS GURU**

Admittedly when I realised my chances to study as a Doctor were shot to pieces despite my good intentions, years of study and perseverance, I thought my life would never be the same and all else would be second best.

How wrong was I? There are so many doctors out there that hate what they are now doing…but 7 years of hard study at University keeps them doing what they have realised isn't the career for them. Dr Edward De Bono is a doctor that changed his career-path. From a long line of GP's it was almost 'expected' that he too follow in the family tradition. He realised after several years as a practicing GP he would be happier helping more people with their way of 'thinking' than by practicing medicine and so became an author and speaker. He chose his road to happiness rather than a burden to be endured, as did Dr John Demartini.

With my bubbly personality and passion to help people I may too have been frustrated only helping one person at a time – in fact the thought of all the blood and gore makes me feel queasy. Instead now I am helping millions through my speaking, books and TV shows ... and I didn't have to study medicine for 7 years to make a difference in their lives ... my years of study are in the countries and from the people of the world. Don't misunderstand me, there are many doctors making in-roads and saving and helping millions with their research work and loving every minute or enjoying the personal contact making a difference one person at a time. We need their skills and expertise and I am sure you and me both are grateful they are there doing an amazing job.

The door of opportunity to becoming a doctor had closed for me, but gee the new door that opened in the field of Travel was great fun.

When I didn't get the grades to go to university to study medicine, the door of opportunity opened to study Pharmacy, which I didn't want to do. I applied to work at one of England's largest travel tour operators, 'Intasun', a company that one of my best friends Susan had been working for since she left school at 16 years old. She had already been abroad 10 times in the past two years with compliments of the company. She loved it. Perhaps I would too!

I had no regrets in joining the world of travel. My interest in people and places made me exceptionally helpful and informative to the travel agents, who had so many queries. I was soon noticed by management and was then asked to attend many public relations launches with hoteliers, top agencies and airlines. I loved the style and glamour and the luxury of travel. I became significant for my people skills and personal standards. I had the opportunity to meet heads of hotel chains and the CEO's of airlines and top management; people with vision, power and a desire to service their clients within their industry. I learnt very quickly to raise my standards of excellence to be like them.

An opportunity arose where I was invited to become the PR person for a 5 star hotel in Majorca Spain. At 18 years old this was an opportunity of a lifetime. I could speak two languages very well, but I was not as brilliant as some of the girls in my grammar school, which had gone to university to study languages so that they could apply for such a 'dream job'. I was thrilled it was being offered to me.

Other doors were also opening. As life would have it – nothing for ages and then 3 possibilities appear at the same time – adding confusion and uncertainty to the equation!

Now I could stay at the present company and move into the computer department and utilise some of my academic skills and still go on trips, study journalism at the university part-time or fly off and live in a beautiful hotel in the sunshine and 'play hostess' to the many guests as a PR person. Option 3 was to go to University and study a Bachelor of Science Degree.

All choices were exciting with great potential. If I had chosen from my heart, I would have gone for the PR job in Spain, but I took the advice of my family and made the decision to stay in the UK and move into the computer department and gain new IT skills that stood me in excellent stead to apply to university to study a Bachelor of Science Degree.

TIP

We never make the wrong decisions, we just make choices that allow us to learn and experience life in different ways and sequences.

**SHELLEY SYKES
THE HAPPINESS GURU**

I did wonder what it would have been like to work as a Hotel PR Manager, but as the universe will have it – if that was what I was meant to do, the opportunity would arise later.

Voilá! It did 6 years later! I ended up working in a 5 star hotel in Crete as PR and Entertainments Manager hosting celebrities and dignitaries from around the world, including the United Nations delegates. It was brilliant and I was far more capable to serve, than perhaps I would have been years earlier.

TIP

*Call it fate or divine planning, but if you are meant to experience something or someone those experience opportunities will appear in your life at **the right time** – not always your planned time.*

**SHELLEY SYKES
THE HAPPINESS GURU**

As I say, nothing is ever wrong. What ever we decide is just perfect and our whole life experiences, becomes our classroom. The doors of opportunity never cease to open.

I worked for a year and then applied to University.

Before starting at University in the UK to study a BSc IT degree, I flew to South Africa on a holiday paid for by my parents for my 18th birthday. Whilst there; opportunity knocked at my door, this time in the form of a lady saying that in IT (Information Technology), a degree was second to experience and that I would be better off 'working' in IT and studying at Open University to get my degree. She mentioned that the Standard Bank of South Africa were recruiting new IT people and were also great at in-house training.

I had a window of opportunity. Now, whilst still in South Africa on holiday was my opportunity to apply for the job, not 6,000 miles away from the UK. I typed up my CV.

On my last day in Johannesburg I went for an interview with the Standard Bank for a job with them and the IT Director offered me a position in operations! They even offered to pay for my visas and transfer to South Africa. I was thrilled.

TIP

We create our own magic by taking ACTION first. The universe conspires then to create the possibilities.

SHELLEY SYKES
THE HAPPINESS GURU

Working for Intasun Tours had been brilliant experience for me and management had been so supportive. They tempted me with several opportunities to stay, which I appreciated, but 6 months later I arrived in Johannesburg aged 19 a new immigrant and an employee of the bank, with temporary lodgings, booked on an Open University course and enrolled at an independent school for computer programming.

Life was exciting and full of possibility. **I was starting to trust my heart more now, rather than think with my head, following my own dreams.** Yee haa!

I was on my own in a new country where I was still seen to be a minor, making adult choices about my own life. The freedom was thrilling. It could have been scary and frightening and for most people their focus on 'what could go wrong' would have overwhelmed them or just frightened them off even attempting to leave, but I chose to see this as a new exciting episode.

**TIP**

My philosophies being: feel the fear and do it anyway. Why worry about the un-known, just expect the best and handle the situations as they come.

SHELLEY SYKES
THE HAPPINESS GURU

Shit Happens

As is apparent throughout my life and most peoples – nothing is ever straightforward. Just weeks before my

departure for South Africa I decided to visit some of my college friends, who had already begun their university courses in the UK. I wanted to say my farewells. I drove down in the car I had just sold, but could keep until my departure, with my suitcase full of my new clothes I had specifically built up ready to take with me to South Africa. I had arrived late and my friends had arranged to take me to a party at their campus. So I didn't unpack the car to my regret, because when we arrived back that evening my car had been broken into and all my personal belongings had long gone. My precious things – some impossible to replace, since I had been buying them from my trips around Europe!

A weekend ruined, because of my loss and focus on what had been and not 'how lucky I was' being there then amongst friends. You could say I was very unhappy. I probably didn't handle my loss well at all because I placed so much attachment to my 'things' – especially clothes and shoes because I had such a penchant for them. Trust me, when I say I am a real girlie girl. I just love shoes!

Now, if that same incident happened to me today, because I have been contaminated with **The Happiness Bug** I would shrug my shoulders and say 'may the people benefit from the luxury of wearing my beautiful outfits' and I would look forward to purchasing and building up a new selection of outfits!

The end result is still the same, yet I would 'feel much happier'.

Life in South Africa

I arrived in South Africa with very few clothes! So what!

Like a magical series of events or doors opening, you could say that:

- If I hadn't moved to SA and worked at the bank I wouldn't have been head hunted by IBM and told to do an MBA, becoming one of their high earning achievers and specialised in marketing and sales.
- If I hadn't done an MBA I wouldn't have gotten my next job as directors assistant to the head of South Africa's largest tour operator, Uniworld Tours.
- If my boyfriend at the time hadn't moved to Cape Town I wouldn't have been entered into the South African **dance competition** by girlfriends trying to cheer me up and as a result won a TV and modelling contract, which gave me experience and a taste for the world of TV and film.
- If I hadn't transferred to Cape Town to manage Uniworld's offices without telling my boyfriend I wouldn't have found him in bed with another woman!
- If that hadn't happened, I wouldn't have focused my life around work and worked as hard, organising weekend trips to Knysna for all the Cape travel agents, who then passed all their business my way.
- If those trips hadn't generated so much business for the companies in Knysna I wouldn't have been **invited to work** for Southern Seas Charter Company as their **PR Manager** and lived and worked in one of South

Africa's most beautiful resorts and learnt how **to skipper a yacht and water ski.**

- If I hadn't moved there I may not have contracted spinal and cerebral meningitis, **nearly dying** and decided life was too short and decided to travel and see the rest of the world, valuing time and ensuring I fill mine with people and experiences.

Life in Malawi

- If I hadn't produced the brochures for Malawi and sold more holidays there than anyone in the country, then I may not have **lived on Lake Malawi** for 3 months and taken people scuba diving on a catamaran with a gorgeous man, before travelling to Greece.

Life in Crete

- I wouldn't have been **United Nations Hostess** if I hadn't accepted the position as PR and Entertainments Manager for a 5 star hotel and mixed and mingled with stars and celebrities, who inspired me to get back into TV.
- If my parents hadn't decided to split then I may not have moved back to the UK to set up my own **travel company and fax business and register with a TV agency** when I did, to be reasonably close to support my mum.

Life back in UK

- If I had been allowed to buy a house as an entrepreneur, I may not have gone back into the world of IT where I met my **first husband** for IBM's largest software company Bluebird.
- If I hadn't lost lots of weight, then I wouldn't have opened Yorkshires **largest Health Spas** and gone back into TV, Speaking and journalistic work.
- If I hadn't travelled to **Holland**, whilst pregnant I may not have been involved in a car accident.
- If my son hadn't **been born blind with cerebral palsy** then perhaps my marriage may have lasted longer, perhaps I would not have become the motivated passionate carer, philanthropist and mother I am today...
- If I hadn't become a specialist in massage therapies and other techniques perhaps my son wouldn't be walking and seeing today.
- If my husband had been a more affectionate great dad my son and I wouldn't have been able to **move to Australia.**

Life In Australia

- If I hadn't had my **hair burnt off my head** at one of Sydney's leading hair dressers before a TV show audition then I may not have had time to **publish my first book,** *Callum's Cure* and get testimonials from royalty to Robbins.
- If I hadn't written the book perhaps **Edward de Bono** wouldn't have read it and nicknamed me '**The Happiness Guru'**

- If I hadn't **lost my investment money** then I may not have been so creative to open **Forever Young Anti-Aging Clinics, write more books, speak, present.**
- If, despite all the shit, I hadn't had so much **luck** I may not have persevered with my dream goals to Make **A** Difference in peoples lives, boosting self-esteem and confidence and walk my talk as **The Happiness Guru,** 'Happiness is an attitude and not what happens to you . . .'

In hindsight our lives are so perfectly mapped out and everything seems to have been a 'force for good' leading us on a journey to where we were meant to be.

Our Futures

With this in mind our future can be equally exciting and less fearful. Because **everything is all right,** I quite happily **take on life with a smile** knowing that it is another lesson on my journey. I know where I want to go and I have an idea how that could go, but now I enjoy the path's twist and turns and **little or big surprises.** That is why, when I am faced with something 'big' I just tell myself 'all is well' and ask myself '**will this matter in a years time?'**

The answer is often 'no' because life rights it's self and goes onwards and upwards. **You could call this my faith, that the universe or God will provide all that I need and more.**

TIP

*By being grateful for all that is **going right** at the present time, keeps the fear at bay and my disposition bright and 'happy'.*

SHELLEY SYKES
THE HAPPINESS GURU

We know that doors can close so living in gratitude right now for everything in our lives at the present time can be a blessing, because when we move on we will have no regrets. **New doors** lead to **new friends, new places, new lives** sometimes and **new ways** of doing things.

We cannot deny that as time marches on so must our lives otherwise we start moving backwards.

TIP

With a happy heart our futures are always brighter than our pasts and our present is just a perfect gift.

SHELLEY SYKES
THE HAPPINESS GURU

As one door closes another opens, brighter than before!

What I suggest you do now is list as I have just done above in bullet form, the path your life has taken so far and ask is it on track to where you want to be? Look back and see where you were mad, bad, depressed or delighted. Looking back now and seeing how things have turned out in the long run have been a benefit rather than a burden and a joy because of the person you have become – awesome.

Now is a time to pat yourself on the back and congratulate yourself for taking the opportunities that you did take and increasing your skill at worrying less and opening more doors!

Looking back I realised that **I spent too long** moping over lost loves, next time I will give myself one week and then celebrate in the adventure of finding a new love!

Looking back I realise that **I took work and what people said personally.** Now and in the future I will listen and only accept that which makes me happy and dismiss that that doesn't.

When we **focus on the loss or lack**, looking at the closed door, we just don't see all the opportunities or doors that open around us. **Anyone** even the optimistic, **get depressed** if they focus on what is WRONG.

I suggest instead of worrying and crying over what once was, **rejoice in the possibility** that that has brought and the excitement of new opportunities and adventures. It's another step closer to our dreams.

As Buddha said to a disciple:
"If I have a gift and you do not accept the gift, whom does the gift belong to?"
The disciple answered "To you Buddha, the gift bearer."

"Correct." Said Buddha. "If I give you an insult, but you do not accept the insult, then to whom does the insult belong?

"To the one that gave the insult" replied the disciple.

"Yes, we have the **choice to take gifts or insults**, but remember the person giving the gift or insult keeps it, if we choose not to accept his kindness (or meanness and then he suffers at his own deed)."

Self Protection

I **never choose to accept insults** or condemnations. I place a bubble around myself, I listen and I choose not to accept for my own confidence and sanity.

That does not mean to say that if I ask for advice I will not take it, but if I feel I or my work is being 'attacked' then I move away and find people that can see my potential and work with my skills.

 **TIP**

We can not be and do everything perfectly, but we can chose to be around people who like us as we are right now and grow and develop with us over time.

SHELLEY SYKES
THE HAPPINESS GURU

Edward de Bono's comments

The world is to be regarded as an opportunity for happiness, not a burden to be endured. Individual situations are to be regarded as full of opportunity rather than full of threatening pressures. Seeking out the opportunities or making the perceptual change necessary may require effort, but that is part of the activity of life. On the other hand, no one should be bullied by opportunity, bullied by the need to make the best possible choice, bullied by the need to get the best possible deal. There has to be the practical application of trade-offs and cut-offs.

No one can do everything or know everything or be perfect.

52

All things bright and beautiful
All creatures great and small,
All things wise and wonderful
the Lord God made them all.

Hymn

chapter 3

How to catch the Happiness Bug

 **TIP**

*Happiness, the most contagious and sought after disease to catch. It is referred to as the Happiness Syndrome, spread by **the Happiness Bug**.*

**SHELLEY SYKES
THE HAPPINESS GURU**

Happiness is...
Knowing without knowing everything will all work out.

Happiness is...
An attitude – we can choose to be happy despite our circumstances

Happiness is...
Living in gratitude every day. Being grateful for all the people, things and possibilities that are great in our lives right now.

Happiness is...
Waking up every morning – alive and well.

Happiness is...
Realising that you are lovable and loving.

Happiness is . . .
Waking up to the sunshine and knowing that the weekend is fast approaching!

Happiness is . . .
Having a big dream and knowing that one day you will realise it.

Happiness is . . .
Being with friends that cherish you just the way you are.

Happiness is . . .
Being able to dance around the room to your favorite music.

The list can go on and certainly does in my book '*Inspirational Words*' – one message for each day of the year or as many as it takes to cheer you up and get you to feel grateful.

Really what is 'happiness' and how can you 'catch **The Happiness Bug?**'

Well after years of experience it dawned on me that it was down to our own perceptions. Happiness is an attitude.

Attitudes are learned skills. We are not born happy or sad. We are not born with an attitude. We are very emotional and it is a feeling of 'happiness' that we enjoy and remember in a positive way.
Yet two people can experience the same experience and 'choose to feel differently about it'. **So one way of catching The Happiness Bug is down to selectively choosing to 'feel' and experience the 'positive happy' feeling out of each situation that gives us the Happiness Syndrome.**

I was at dinner with friends at Easter and they were experiencing a tough time emotionally and financially, because my friend Nick had not secured work since his last contract ended pre-Christmas and the finances and his confidence were seeping away. The conversation touched on happiness, balance and reality. His partner Lisa was saying how proud she was that he was handling his problems so well. Life is a balance.

My illusion was that Nick was, despite being a positive person, feeling the fear and it was clinging to his aura and I really wanted to help him shed that fear that was possibly holding him back. There are many ways to look at his situation. I described 2 possible options to him.

Option one:
- He is out of work.
- Living in a property he doesn't own.
- Has twin sons that he hardly ever sees.
- Finances are tight.
- Short listed for a job with the CEO backing the other fellow.
- Living with a woman that has high expectations and doesn't work...

No wonder the guy has fears and doubts – anyone would.

Option two:
- He could use this time to rest and revitalise himself.
- Reinvent who he wants to be. Sort out his filing systems etc.
- He is healthy and good-looking.

- His environment is plush. He is living in a beautiful home that is beautifully decorated.
- He has twin boys that when he does see them, are delighted to be in his company, unlike most teenagers and their parents.
- He doesn't have to put up with all their teenage issues.
- He is a millionaire without the cash flow at the moment.
- He is intelligent, smart, enthusiastic, a leader.
- There are so many possibilities of work here and abroad.
- Soon to be the winner of the job offer, because his direct boss wants him.
- He has the love and support of a sexy, loving and lovable woman who respects and admires him.
- Dining with great caring supportive friends, who like him for him.

Both options are valid and true. The second option list sounds more exciting and up lifting. The Happiness Guru would choose **only to view** the second option. Why? Because the air of depression, desperation, despondency is lifted and hope and belief and gratitude for what is 'right' is still there.

As I said there are other options and I got the idea that Nick goes by a third option, a combination of one and two, yo-yoing between the two for 'balance'!

Let me tell you this is not necessary at all. When shit happens it has happened – that is the one dark side. By thinking positively, you are balancing out the shit . . . you **don't have to** create waves by throwing your own yin-yang stuff in, to balance it even more!

TIP

It is simple. Be happy and expectant of great things. Look not at the door that has shut, but at all the new doors that are open and opening.

SHELLEY SYKES
THE HAPPINESS GURU

Spookily enough, the next time I called at their house, Lisa was initially on her own. We had only just started pleasantries when Nick walked in looking divine in a tailored suit, tall and squared with a massive smile on his face. He had just secured the job he was and had been hoping for, with one of the major banks in the city. I was thrilled and relieved for him. It had been a while coming – persistence had paid dividends. He said it was a shock when he got the news a bit like a prisoner that had been left to rot in prison and then suddenly, unexpectedly told he was free to leave...
Nick earnestly told me that he had watched a film about the famous French prisoner Dreyfuss, who was falsely accused of espionage in the late 1890s. He was sent to rot in jail on Devil's Island after a Life sentence was passed. Life meant 'Life', as it so often does for ourselves. But the Universe sent a gift that was invisible to Dreyfuss in the form of Emile Zola, who famously wrote *j'accuse* in taking on the 'honour' of the entire French army. After many years of persistence to clear Dreyfuss's good name. Zola triumphed against the odds. Dreyfuss was finally exonerated and pardoned. The prison guards opened Dreyfuss's cell door and in a matter-of-fact way they said "You are free to go!" They both left leaving Dreyfuss's free to leave. And yet Dreyfuss stood still in absolute disbelief. He was still a

prisoner in his own mind. Finally he left his cell and felt the breeze of fresh air on his face and only then felt free. Like Nick says "In truth, it was only his own permission that granted himself the right to leave. So many of us don't realise that we make our own prisons and that tragically we are our own gaolers."

Nick had stood there not sure if it was safe to take a step towards the door. Of course it was only a fleeting moment before he jumped for joy and the reality hit. He had a job! Now you might say 'gee how can you stop the fear or misery welling up inside when you are not as focused on all the positive aspects?' Or 'how do you cope when more 'stuff' continues to be thrown at you and it starts to mount up?'

We all have problems. I remember one day last October when I was at some highway traffic lights on my way home from a meeting in the city, when a bus started to reverse into me – or more appropriately over the top of my Porsche convertible. I saw my life flash before my eyes, I had the roof down and I was being concertinaed between the bus and the big Four-wheel drive behind me. I 'pipped' the horn, but the driver didn't hear – thankfully the bus' screaming passengers alerted the bus driver that he was just about to decapitate 'Penelope Pit Stop' in her little ol' car.

If that wasn't bad enough, the four-wheel drive owner was sick of the delay and rammed his way out of the pile up and dinged my door. Driving home after all the kafuffle and the exchange of details with witnesses and drivers, I was nearly home, only 5 kilometres to go, when my dinted car thumped down into a large pothole in the road, snapping my exhaust in half! Sparks flashed and the screeching of metal on the road and the throttle of the exhaust was deafening. I managed to crawl to a garage, whose mechanics kindly removed my exhaust. They couldn't repair it, but at least I would get home...yes, sounding like a kamikaze jet fighter plane! Everyone turned his or her heads to look, when I drove past.

I have never sat so low in my sporty seats as I did that day!

I was emotionally drained from the experiences of the day. After cooking and doing the chores like a good parent, I decided it was far better to have a bath and have a good nights rest...

I read my son a chapter from one of the books we were reading and returned to the lounge to find it flooded with water. I had forgotten to turn off the bath water!

That night I was still scooping up water at past midnight... the neighbour and I emptied over 120 buckets of water from the carpet washing machine... I was on the second floor apartment – the neighbours below and to the side of me were also flooded... I was not popular! I was so very tired.

I could have asked 'why me?' but I didn't.

That day:

- I was grateful that people were kind enough to be witnesses to my car accident.
- I was grateful that I was alive and could get home to my son.
- I was grateful to the garage who took off my exhaust and stored it for me until the repairer could pick it up.
- I was grateful that I owned a carpet washing machine.
- I was grateful that I had a neighbour who offered to help me scoop up the water.

There was so much to be grateful for and I went to bed feeling exhausted, but happy – another adventurous day!

You must admit, I could have been pretty down. The negatives if I had chosen to focus on them, could have had me spiral down with despondency and then depression. Instead the negatives that happened evoked the gratitude and joy within me. I felt lucky, happy to be alive and loved by people that cared.

The result was that I was delighted that my carpets were now clean, the exhaust had been fixed and checked and the car resprayed, looking like new and I had another great story to tell. Ok so there were lots of paper work, time down without a car etc, but that brought it's own reasons to be grateful.

There are other ways to help you become grateful or feel happier about situations too.

Do things that purposefully give us the happy feeling.

For example when I am feeling blue all I have to do is switch on some happy hip hop **music** and before I know it, I am singing along and my state has changed in an instant. If I go **dancing** I lose myself in the rhythm and lose all my worries. I love to dance and I just can't stay miserable when I am on the dance floor. **Walking** has the same effect for many too.

It has been proven that when you **laugh** or **sing** your vibrational energy increases. Anna in the movie 'The King and I' told her son to **'sing or whistle a happy tune'** when ever he was feeling scared or blue. It works.

For those of you who can't sing there is the 'Be Happy Energising Spray' that increases your vibration level to the maximum. A friend of mine created a spray using special ingredients including essential oils that when sprayed behind the neck and head has been proven to lift the persons energies and can actually be photographed. With a few modifications the 'Be Happy Energising Spray' was created to enhance peoples moods and energy levels after just spraying behind the neck and head. It can be purchased www.shelleysykes.com and is simply a must when you are tired or just need that little help.

Happy Habits

In this chapter we are going to go through a few techniques that will create new 'Happy Habits©', but first you need to make a list of all the things you do or can do, to change your state from one less positive to one of happiness for example:

Bush walk,
Stroll on the beach,
Go fishing,
Play on your Play Station,
Make-love (cor I wish),
Dance,

Sing,
Kick a ball,
Play golf,
Horse Ride,
Drive a car,
Spring clean,
Sit by the sea,
Read a trashy novel,
Read an Inspirational Words of wisdom book (mine is available!)
Go to a psychic,
Yoga,
Polish your car,
Sit at your favourite café and sip your drink-watching people
    pass by,
Play an instrument,
Paint,
Write,
Phone a friend,
Eat chocolate cake,
Watch a comedy,
Shop,
Lunch with friends,
Work out in the gym,
Jog,
Stroke your cat,
Cycle,
Sleep,
Look up at the sky,
Speak to a mentor,
Chant a mantra,
Meditate,

Hang out with friends,
Sail,
Motorbike ride,
Skateboard,
Surf,
Play basketball,
Book a holiday,
Count your cash,
Smell the roses,
Spray 'Be Happy Energising Spray',
Water the garden,
Pamper yourself,
Spend time with your family,
Get away from your family,
Positive self-talk,
Look at your list of achievements to date,
Fix, glue, and mend,
Cook...

Your list can comprise of a long list or you may have just one or two, as long as those things, or actions bring a smile to your 'dial'. There will be 'something' that makes you 'feel' good no matter what is happening in your life.

Now with your list in front of you rate how easily you can do that thing that makes you happy from 1 to 10 for example. Music is accessible nearly everywhere for me at home, work and in the car. With my Apple Ipod anywhere any time I can have music. So as soon as I play happy music I start to feel happy...so I would give that a 9 or 10. Even if I sing I start to feel happier, where as sitting by the sea may take a while to get to or won't be appropriate for where I am at...so I may have to give it a 4 since I live near the sea, but it isn't as convenient.

Here are the 9 Tips to Happiness

1. Have a 'Happy Plan'

Preparation is everything because lets face it when we are 'not feeling' happy then it isn't always easy to think straight or creatively. If we feel down and 'know' that music up-lifts us then we can choose to switch on the music and lift ourselves out of our 'down mood'. Once our mood lifts then we can focus on what is 'right' and work out what could be the positive out of our situation. **It's that simple.**

2. Attitude – Smiling

Let's try a practical test. Stand in front of a mirror and smile – looking at your-self whilst smiling, try and attempt to feel sad!

You can't can you? It is impossible to feel sad, whilst you are smiling!

I love to smile. People always smile back – **always!**

Try it next time you are out. Smile at everyone that you pass. You will want to laugh out aloud, because it is like magic. Some people even talk to you!

When you are feeling low, one of your action plans could be to put a smile on your face – like an actor. Spookily that smile takes over your body and once again you begin to feel happier!

It is the universal language of a positive greeting for humans globally. Two foreigners may not be able to speak each other's language, but if they smile at one another they assume that each is friendly and open.

Sexy Singles are advised to smile a lot, because a smile attracts people to you – that means your soul mate! Most **Lucky-in-Loves** are much happier than their single counterparts, they live longer lives, are healthier and have a higher vibration (it's obvious that it must be the regular sex!), but seriously, their communication and connection is what keeps them buoyant. They are not so self-critical. So smile and attract your happy soul mate for increased vitality and a balanced and passionate sex life. If you need tips get my *Sexy Single and Ready to Mingle* book! It works! We even have a 'Sexy Magnetising Spray' to increase your energy vibrational levels so that you can be even more appealing. www.shelleysykes.com

3. Physiology – Walk Tall

Our physiology plays a massive part in our attitude, if we stand tall and straight, we feel 'better'. Only when we are slumped do we feel low and down! An easy way to become uplifted in our emotions is by standing tall and smiling. You also look slimmer too – so it's just a must!

Body movement is a sure way to increase your happiness quotient. Depressed people move at a much slower pace and seem to look down a lot. Happy focused people look straight a head and walk with a brisk pace. I'm even known to skip, even at my age! Remember Peter Pan and Tinker Bell never stopped skipping! Who cares what anyone thinks, just do what makes 'you happy' and the world will follow in your footsteps.

I will discuss health and image in more detail in the proceeding chapters, because without your health how can you enjoy your happiness to the full and lets face it, most happy people are healthier people too and we will find out how and why.

4. Surround yourself with High-Energy People

I personally love to connect with others when I am happy and as we have said happiness is contagious.

When we are around happy people our energy is lifted and we too feel empowered and energised.

Happy people certainly have high-energy vibrational readings. Look at your friends and family. Do they empower you? Are they constantly bringing you down and draining your energies? If they do, move out of home, get new friends . . . it's time to move on and up! It's harsh reality, but if you stick around 'down people' they end up bringing you down. You can't uplift them for long. **It is my belief that two people coming together should boost one another and become a better whole.**

Sometimes your family are controlling and have low self-esteem or they fear that you will get hurt if you follow your dreams and don't make it, so they try and dissuade you from trying.

TIP

*According to old people, it is better to try and aim high
than live in regret and wonder what if!
If you can dream you can achieve!
Anything is possible.*

**SHELLEY SYKES
THE HAPPINESS GURU**

So look around and see which of your friends are supportive and inspirational and start hanging out with those people.

It is an old saying **'show me a man's friends and I will tell you about the man'**. The people we mix with define us! We become like the people we associate with. Spooky, but true.
Exciting people have exciting friends.

If you want to be happy, hang out with happy people. If you want to be rich and happy, hang out with **rich happy people** – trust me they do exist! Millions of them!

Mirror what 'happy', people do, say, dress, think and behave like. It can be exciting and fun. There are of course many rich, unhappy people, but they have one difference and that is their attitude or lack of it. Let's face it, there are happy, poor people, who appreciate their life despite their financial restraint and there are very unhappy people who have the same issues who believe if they had more money then they would be happy. The wealthy people who have succeeded financially, who have it all, love, luck, lifestyle and lolly have chosen to appreciate all that they have in their lives and have obviously caught **The Happiness Bug.**

They know it isn't the things in life that make them happy, but their appreciation that they can choose to be happy from within. They are grateful for everything right now and chose to be gentle and loving with themselves and those around them.

5. Ideas – Abundance mentality

Happy people come from an understanding of **abundance** and not scarcity. The greatest wealth really comes from ideas. Making those ideas come to life. We all have ideas. Only a few act on them.

The ONE difference between a poor man and a wealthy one is LUCK. They say we make our own luck. I believe Luck has four parts:

L – Location
U – Understanding
C – Commitment/Connections/Communication
K – Knowledge

A man with an idea in Uganda may have less opportunity to market or sell his idea than one in Asia . . . but then again it might be more appropriate for the idea to be in Uganda. There are many people in Uganda who are extremely wealthy. **Location** does have an impact on feasibility.

To understand the needs of others and to be able to offer a solution for their benefit is key to success too.

Passion, persistence, commitment to an idea, plan or project and to be able to **communicate** to others what you have on offer is important too. Its no good having a great idea or product or service if no one knows about it. Your **connections** or their connections help get that message out. You don't have to do it all on your own.

Finally it comes down to **knowledge.** You don't need to know everything but you need to know someone who has got that knowledge or where to go to find out. The Internet is the first place people research these days. It is such an amazing tool. Most wealthy people rate their team as the highest resource they have. John Paul Getty, one of the wealthiest men in the US last century stated he would rather have 100 people working for him than commit 100 hours of his own time that could best be utilised thinking up new ideas.

On the TV show 'Dragon's Den' about millionaire investors helping small business people create their dream by investing in their ideas, state to have a great business one needs:

- Financial backing
- A great support team
- A great idea or business plan

When I personally started to research other successful people, I realised that **no one had done it on their own.** They had all either had a mentor or a financial backer or someone who believed in their dream or idea or given them a lift up the ladder.

I read the *One Minute Millionaire* by Jack Cranfield, whom suggested that we all need to go out and find a millionaire as a mentor to help us develop our millionaire strategies. I was lucky. I had been introduced to a 'billionaire' who found millions 'boring'! He was a 68-year-old Yorkshire man that had moved to Australia as a young man. After struggling in Tasmania in the property market, he sought to make his wealth in Sydney and arrived with only $50. He loved property and to negotiate. He found a property that needed renovation and then sat by a phone and rang every banker, financier in town until he found one that loved his idea, passion and zest to renovate and sell to a different clientele.

Offering a 50% return on his investment Bernard Lewis began his climb to the top of Australian property league. His advice to me before he died was not to worry about what percentage of your idea you were giving away or sharing, but to get it into motion. When your idea works people start wanting to throw money at your next ideas, projects and plans and there are always more ideas, projects and plans to follow the first.
His sound advice seems to ricochet with so many successful people.

Walt Disney as we all know, had one of the biggest, best, most exciting ideas and with only $5 left in his pocket he continued to knock on the doors of the big investors, not accepting rejection personally, he persisted until one man finally agreed to finance his dream project Disney Land, which then became a reality for us all.

Richard Branson is one of the richest men in the world and I believe from meeting him, one of the happiest. He lives in gratitude and appreciates all that he has created. He is aware of the power that his possessions bring and uses that power in the force for good. He is a great philanthropist and takes pleasure in helping others achieve their dreams, whilst still following his own. He is definitely a people's person and realises his strength is in his people and the people around the world.

He still loves the challenges life throws at him and understands life is a constant lesson. I was thrilled to see his zest for life and his humbleness. A great man we can all emulate and look up to because he is truly being himself for himself. He is shining his light and allowing others to do the same.

6. Live in the Now

There is a saying that the past is long gone, tomorrow is an unknown future, but **the present is the gift that can be enjoyed right now.** I love gifts. 'Right now' is so very special – it is life. Just stop for a moment and just savour this moment . . . you are obviously reading this book . . . where are you, are you comfortable, somewhere lovely and exotic or curled up in bed at home, lying next to someone – so give them a kiss?

I am lying in bed; it's 10 am – what luxury, with my laptop rested against my knees in my 'Princess Shelley bed' plumped up with a heap of pretty cushions. I have sunshine beaming through my windows, blue skies, the scent from the flowers in the vase facing my bed is filling the room with a delicious sweet aroma, my son's computer is zapping and whirring in the distant back ground and I am feeling happy and content as the words just spill out on to this page. I feel lucky I have this time right now to type before the 'normal routine begins' – all is well, at peace, safe and exciting, because I know that this book will touch you in some inspirational way.

The present is all we have right now. **So happy people just focus on right now and experience the joy that this moment is bringing.**

- **Does it matter** right now as you are reading this book if you have millions in the bank or not? No.
- **Does it matter** as you are reading this book if you have found your soul mate or not? No.
- **Does it matter** if right now, you are a little overweight, spotty, too thin, can't afford a 'thingy-ma-gig' or not? No.

Right now you are enjoying down time for yourself. You are investing in yourself so that you can enjoy more of the happy you and by being the happy you, make a difference to others. How exciting is that!

Worry leads to fear and the fear of possibilities is more frightening than facing the thing we are worrying about. As the song says:

> "Don't worry, be happy"

It has become a habit for many of us to worry, because our parents have taught us and we hear it time and time again... I worry about you... I'm worried about the...

 **TIP**

Worry is the most useless, ineffective waste of our gift, our present time.

SHELLEY SYKES
THE HAPPINESS GURU

By being present you can appreciate the people, the place, the experiences and the journey right now as it is. Right now my environment could be like that of Jackie Collins equivalent, in her mansion in Hollywood writing her next best seller – at the other side of the world here I am luxuriating in opulence writing a world best seller – soul touching stuff that's easy to read like Jackie's sexy stuff.

Ok, so I don't have her maids making lunch downstairs, but I'm not hungry at the moment. I don't have her millions in the bank, but who needs millions to do what I am doing right now – writing. So back to my 'Happy Present' this glamorous writer, me laying in the princess bed, typing, whilst my son is happily kept busy on his computer, the flowers continue to fill the air in my designer, immaculately clean apartment and whilst the sun continues to shine through my windows . . . it's glorious!

7. Expect the best

A **Happy Habit**, which is just a must, is to expect the best. Some people think that that will bring bad karma or it is tempting fate. If you are not happy most of the time and you want to be, then change and expect the best from now on.

A common factor between highly successful happy people **is they expect to win, succeed, be happy, be the best at what they do, achieve their goal, be lucky** . . . it just is.

If you count up all the 'unlucky' things that have ever happened to me I am probably **one of the unluckiest** people; I have ever met. Car crashes, divorce, disabled child, major financial loss, sickness, near death experiences . . .

In fact, however I tell everyone I am one of the **luckiest people I know**. I have had some amazing things happen to me in my life – just the people that I get to meet is pretty awesome and lucky really, to travel to places like the Antarctica on a cruise ship is pretty lucky, to swim in volcanoes and live in a place where the parrots live freely and not in cages is pretty cool and where it is only a couple of hours drive away from a place where my son and I can swim freely with Dolphins.

Most **successful people have had more failures** than most people. Why? because they try more things and go for what ever they are aiming for. If you think you will succeed, you go for it. If you don't expect to succeed why try at all? Most people don't even begin to try. Remember Thomas Edison who invented the light bulb. It took 10,000 experiments before it finally worked. He did it! Most unsuccessful people would have quit. **If you quit you are guaranteed to fail. If you persist you are guaranteed an interesting journey.**

Remember it is better to try and fail than not try at all and live in regret. **If you expect the best then of course you are going to embark on a new adventure and see where it takes you. It's a numbers game and in the end you come up smelling of roses, a winner! Nothing ventured is ever wrong. Taking the risk in a venture is quite a ride.**

8. Focus on being Successful

Happy people are definitely focused. Wether it is to be a loving partner, parent, a mother or a business man on a mission to make a difference to how people think, work, do things, enjoy themselves or whole combinations of things. Our dreams are what make us unique and literally shine our light. It is often called living in the flame. It is that 'je ne sais pas' as the French say, 'I don't know what' that ignites us up and on. A passion to be or do something that excites us inside. It is different for each one of us. It is a dream, an idea or way of being that suits our personality from the core, rather than has been imposed upon us.

Each person's success is measured by; their own interpretation of 'what success is'. I know a man, Mark who says he is successful when he wakes up every morning and he is alive and well. Just to be above ground is success in his eyes. This man is easily pleased and finds success easily to come by each and every day. Mark is one of the happiest men I know.

There are others who have such high standards of success that they only feel success occasionally. One man, who became a client of mine, said that he only felt successful when each of his employees asks for his help. This is a man with 600 employees, millions in the bank, great wife, kids, holidays, great business, but this man feels unsuccessful because not all his employees asks for his help!
Lets face it, most would avoid asking for the CEO's help just so that they don't look incompetent or not enough for their job. After working out a better success plan this man's

whole persona has shifted. He lives in gratitude with all the things that are going right in his life. The weight of the world has lifted from his shoulders and he is a lot jollier. His new success model is that he feels successful when his staff – 'don't ask' for help, because it means that they are all working well. He still has an open door policy so that they can come to him with their questions and ideas, because he realises he likes to help people and make a difference. So to allow for that we implemented a plan to help his local community by setting up a tithing scheme through 2B1 Charitable Foundation for the company and employees if they wanted to join in making a difference to individuals and groups in their region.

If you notice, nothing really changed in his life except the meaning he was giving to things. When the **meaning changes** in a way that uplifts you, then it can only motivate and inspire you. Good things can then come from this newfound energy and inspiration, such as his company contribution charity fund. I bet he is now much easier to live with and work with. Have you noticed unhappy people are a lot grouchier than happy people?

9. Shine – Enjoy being yourself

Nelson Mandela told us 'who are we not to shine our light!' Sometimes the battle isn't about shining, but just finding the 'light bulb' and the 'switch'. **If you don't know what your purpose in life is or what your special gifts are how then do you know how to shine?**

To some people it is so obvious and to others it is a burden and torment working it out. **Simply put, to shine is to be just who we are and do what we really enjoy being and doing and somehow that magic combination works and inspires others.**
It really is that simple. Truly.

Some say that you need to have grandiose ideas, plans to change the world, but no, that is not true for everyone. Our purpose is JUST TO BE. Being a happy bee is much better than a grumpy bee. We often put restrictions on ourselves such as I will only go to the beach when I have finished this chapter . . . not me if I feel I need to go, I go now, whilst the weather is sunny and I will benefit from the fresh air. I can always come back and type into the night and finish off the chapter when the beach is cold and black.

It's not about doing the right thing for others. It's about doing the right thing for ourselves. We touch and inspire others by being genuine and ourselves.
It took me ages to find it out. After years of trying to please people, being the good girl it never seemed to fully work.

I think the easiest way to 'shine' is to just follow your heart and your gut. Forget logic and your head. If you follow your instincts then the journey will be a much freer experience and more fun. It is certainly easier to be happier when you have to only work out how to keep yourself joyful.

Nelson Mandela was a prisoner in jail for 27 years just for a belief that black and white people should be treated equally. One man locked away. He would not give up his dream and whilst in prison he stayed happy and expectant, because he was being true to himself. It would have been more logical and easier on his family if he had conceded his beliefs, but no, he did it for himself and the result was awesome. When released he was not bitter and twisted. He expected that his dream would become a reality somehow, some day. He probably never dreamed that one day he would become president of his country or a world leader!

Sometimes our dreams become even bigger better realities than we could ever have envisioned.

When Richard Branson first started his Virgin Record Shop he probably never envisioned owning airlines, credit cards and a multitude of other global businesses. He was just doing and being himself, playing records in a place with comfy chairs.

The answer to 'how do I shine?' is: BE YOURSELF and DO what makes you feel happy even when the chips are down.

Edward de Bono's comments

What sort of action can an individual take in order to increase their happiness? There must be an element of awareness of one's own temperament and of past experiences. Skill in happiness is based like any other skill on experience and self-observation. There is a place for the development of willpower and discipline and also for sensitisation through deliberate training.

It is probably not possible ever to induce happiness by an effort of will. But an individual can generate or choose circumstances, which themselves can generate happiness. An individual can also work on his perceptions so that he comes to look at things in a different way. So circumstances can be changed, or the perception of circumstances.

A person dieting can choose either to take a little food or to take a lot and then deliberately leave some on their plate. In the pursuit of happiness there is considerable scope for action and choice. It is not a matter of passively hoping that happiness will happen like a rainbow in the sky.

In happiness, as in cooking there is a brew of ingredients to suit different tastes.

Every individual can construct his own 'happiness profile' based on what he knows of his own personality and the opportunities open to him. Does a person want a steady profile, perhaps even a climbing one? Or does a person want a profile characterised by peaks with the inevitable troughs in between?
The happiness profile can include as much or as little as a person wishes for peace, joy, interest, enthusiasm, pleasure and excitement. It is somewhat like cooking and deciding on the right balance of ingredients to suit a particular taste.

Life is lived in small things and it is around these that happiness must be built rather than on a hoped-for future.

9 Tips to Happiness

1. Have a 'Happy Plan'.
2. Attitude – Smiling.
3. Physiology – Walk tall.
4. Surround yourself with high-energy people.
5. Ideas – Abundance Mentality.
6. Live in the 'Now'.
7. Expect the Best.
8. Focus on being successful.
9. Shine – Enjoy being yourself.

chapter 4

The Happiness Experience

Happiness isn't always about 'feeling joyous all the time', it's about focusing on what is right in your life and what you want more of.

**SHELLEY SYKES
THE HAPPINESS GURU**

Our **happiness experiences** are so often reflected in the way we form our words and state our beliefs. We often have to review those beliefs. Some of our beliefs in the past worked for us and then become redundant and even become a burden to have. We need to enjoy more happy experiences.

Some may criticise us and say that we should feel happy only when it naturally occurs, but if that is so, how much sadder the world will remain. We have already shown one example how one business mans life changed to be a happier one for himself and those around him; just by **changing the meaning** he gave things. If we have the choice to be happy regularly or just sometimes what would your choice be? I am assuming, because you are reading this book your answer is – to be happy.

In the **Happiness Experience** we will be learning simple skills that keep us motivated towards being happy each day. We will find out what our limiting beliefs are so that we can modify them to work for us rather than against ourselves. We all deserve to experience happiness despite our life circumstances and not have to wait for the 'perfect' conditions.

In this chapter I hope that the journey is just as enjoyable and as exciting to you as the end result of feeling the joy.

At a weekend seminar I attended, I was fortunate to get some one-on-one time with the head coach, Dave who had commented on my happy high energy. He also noticed from my stories, that a lot of adventure was created from a single belief I had that 'the universe would come to my rescue **'in the end'**. The way I was manifesting adventure was that everything happened just in the nick of time, at the end. The adventure often came from the ciaos of stress and tensions and living on the edge right **up to the end**. This had worked well for me in the past when something dyer had happened like the birth of my son.

Suddenly it clicked. I got an 'Ah ah' – I was leaving it all to THE END. Yes I loved adventure, the variety, however not the stress of 'last minuteness'. Another possibility for me was to create a '**Happier Experience**' in my life by using the mantra that my life was adventurous, smooth and synchronistic. The universe conspires to work at the right time and at the right place with the right people.' There is no mention of 'in the end.' NOW, **it's at the right time**...

Just the sound of 'synchronistic and smooth' felt like music to my ears. If you notice, that most happy experiences are the simple ones. Seeing someone smile. Smelling grandmas baking. If we can get a series of those simple happy experiences lined up to recall, then we have the secret to enjoying happiness whenever we want.

My new mantra is 'synchronistic and smooth' and I now choose to say these new words, instead of 'the universe would come to my rescue in the end'. It has brought about a new calmness. My life is still full of adventure, that is now in the flow . . . and oh so much easier and yes simpler. I can enjoy the experiences of adventure without experiencing such sharp peaks and troughs. It is at a more enjoyable level. My adrenaline levels are taking a break and I love the smooth ride!

As we have mentioned before we are all different. We have the 9 tips to be happy and now it is time to work out how to apply those 9 tips into our daily life experiences. Now we need to learn how to keep these happy experiences going or in motion.

We can all learn these skills, in fact it is a must, in today's fast paced society where so much can fly by and be missed if effort isn't placed to take the time to experience things that bring us joy.

I have created a questionnaire for you to complete in the 7 areas of your life. I also have a few questions about you personally so that we can highlight any skills and patterns you have that make your life happier and where possibly they can be applied in other parts of your life, where perhaps you need a Happy Habit inserting or perhaps even replacing an out dated one.

Aristotle the Greek philosopher said: "We are what we repeatedly do. Excellence then, is not an act, but a habit."

Happiness Experience Personality Questionnaire

What do you do naturally well, better than most without thinking about it? It could be getting on with people, organising, rapping . . . talents that you have.

____

____

What are you passionate about? It can be anything from caring for pets, creating new ideas, building things, relating to people . . .

____

____

What really excites you and brings meaning to what you do?

____

____

What special knowledge do you have that could help others?

____

____

What positive words would describe your character, your uniqueness, words others would describe you as being.

____

____

What do you want most out of life?

____

____

What makes you special?

____

____

What do you want for this world?

____

____

How happy do you think people see you at the moment?

____

____

How happy would you like them to see you?

____

____

How would you have to **behave** for them to see you like the above?

____

____

What would you have to **think or say to yourself** in order for you to be able to confidently behave that way on a regular basis?

____

____

If everything is possible, what **must you do** to ensure that you say, think and do those things?

____

____

Will this new way of thinking and being still suit your personality?

____

____

(The answer here should be Yes, if not, re-ask the questions again until you get the way of thinking and being to reflect your personality and still match how you want to be perceived.)

Bruce Lee the Kung Fu actor said: "As we think, so shall we become."

Spookily peoples perceptions of how they would like to be perceived is often how they truly are, but they have been hiding their light or criticised so much that they have not blossomed yet.

Now that you have a clearer idea of how you know you can be perceived and it suits your personality and we have an idea of the way one must think in order to be that way – now we can move onto finding where our thoughts are not being congruent with our happy way of being, truly ourselves.

7 Key Areas of Life

Wealth is freedom.
The seven freedoms are:
- Money freedom
- Social freedom
- Time freedom
- Relationship freedom
- Spiritual freedom
- Physical freedom and
- Freedom to pursue your genius.

Health – physical freedom

To enjoy life to the full we need to feel energised and feel well.

How would you rate your health right now from 0 to 10?

____

____

What actions need to be taken to improve?

____

____

If you knew you could not fail what action would you take in the next 30 days?

____

____

If you took these actions how would you feel?

____

____

What rating would you be?

____

____

Social – time freedom

As humans we are connected to others and have a skill and a need to mix and mingle. We all instinctively like making a difference and helping others too.

How would you rate your **social life** right now from 0 to 10?

____

____

What actions need to be taken to improve?

____

____

If you knew you could not fail what action would you take in the next 30 days?

____

____

If you took these actions how would you feel?

____

____

What rating would you be?

____

____

How would you rate your **social contribution** right now from 0 to 10?

____

____

What actions need to be taken to improve?

____

____

If you knew you could not fail what action would you take in the next 30 days?

____

____

If you took these actions how would you feel?

____

____

What rating would you be?

____

____

Relationships – relationship freedom

It is our relationships and connections with ourselves and others that often determine how smooth and successful our life can be. The honesty in open relationships is wonderful and so much easier.

How would you rate your **romantic relationship** right now from 0 to 10?

What actions need to be taken to improve?

If you knew you could not fail what action would you take in the next 30 days?

If you took these actions how would you feel?

What rating would you be?

How would you rate your **work/school relationships** right now from 0 to 10?

____

____

What actions need to be taken to improve?

____

____

If you knew you could not fail what action would you take in the next 30 days?

____

____

If you took these actions how would you feel?

____

____

What rating would you be?

____

____

Finances

Givers Get.

Wealth = Value × Leverage

How would you rate your finances right now from 0 to 10?

____

____

How can your create more value?

____

____

What actions need to be taken to improve?

____

____

If you knew you could not fail what action would you take in the next 30 days?

____

____

If you took these actions how would you feel?

____

____

What rating would you be?

____

____

Family & friends

How would you rate your family relationships right now from 0 to 10?

____

____

What actions need to be taken to improve?

____

____

If you knew you could not fail what action would you take in the next 30 days?

____

____

If you took these actions how would you feel?

____

____

What rating would you be?

____

____

How would you rate your friendships right now from 0 to 10?

____

____

What actions need to be taken to improve?

____

____

If you knew you could not fail what action would you take in the next 30 days?

____

____

If you took these actions how would you feel?

____

____

What rating would you be?

____

____

Spirituality

Belief is a powerful motivator. Feeling or knowing you are not alone can make a massive difference to enjoying being you and taking the risks.

How would you rate your spirituality right now from 0 to 10?

____

____

What actions need to be taken to improve?

____

____

If you knew you could not fail what action would you take in the next 30 days?

____

____

If you took these actions how would you feel?

____

____

What rating would you be?

____

____

Career

Are you already doing what you love and inspires you to get up everyday or are you exchanging your time for money in a job or career you don't really like?

____

____

How would you rate your career right now from 0 to 10?

____

____

What actions need to be taken to improve?

____

____

If you knew you could not fail what action would you take in the next 30 days?

____

____

If you took these actions how would you feel?

____

____

What rating would you be?

____

____

Now these exercises seem to be a lot of work in order to become happy, but as we said before the value you will get by being happier each day is certainly worth reviewing yourself and keeping yourself focused on what it is that really lights you up.

Goethe said:
"Knowing is not enough. We must apply.
Willing is not enough. We must do."

As I have said before if you keep doing the same things you will get the same results. If you want to have a 'happier outcome' then let us look at what we can do.

It makes sense to spend more time doing what we really enjoy. Most people have been misguidedly taught, that they must be practical, only a few people are a success and make loads of money doing what they love doing. These 'doom sayer's' are living in fear of financial security. They are 'what if' people. Sadly people with unlived 'big' dreams.

Most successful people would say they made their fortune doing what they really loved doing. Their focus wasn't on money, but having fun and getting paid for doing something that can ultimately bring benefit to others. Their main aim was to seek pleasure for themselves. A soccer player didn't take up the sport, because of the spectators watching. No, he did it because it was fun. The fact that people are willing to pay to watch the game allows the soccer player to do what he enjoys and get paid for doing it.
Bill Gates loves tinkering and twiddling with computers, creating new software systems that are easier for everyone to connect with one another. Did he set out to make billions

of dollars – no. He just likes creating stuff. I am sure he is thrilled that his systems help millions of people around the world and are practically applied and I am sure he loves the lifestyle his wealth has enabled him to enjoy as well as the great feeling he gets when he donates massive cheques to charities.

Simply put, do what you love doing. Create a new career for yourself doing that. Most nursery schools started with one lady loving being a mum and getting paid for being a great mum to other working mum's kids, allowing others to work because it's what they are good at. Child Day Care is the fastest growing business and very lucrative. My friends George and Adel both have cleaning companies and make a great living cleaning up. In fact I have a friend Lisa, who is a millionairess, because she sorts out all the 'poo' we humans excrete. Her waste recycle company has allowed her to buy a mountain in which to build an eco friendly healing sanctuary for people and families. She loves what she does, has time freedom to be with her son, contribute to society and the world and 'be herself' at home in the mountains.

Our honest open communication starts with ourselves. **We are ALL good at something.** That something is what makes us great and successful. Be proud of being you and congratulate yourself for allowing yourself to be.

I know this all smacks of selfishness – it isn't. To do what makes YOU Happy has a ripple effect and everyone gets contaminated with your joy.

Edward de Bono's comments

Happiness is regarded as the legitimate purpose of man's existence. Happiness is regarded as the proper functioning of the system we call man. To some people it may seem a contradiction in terms that there should be an *effort* towards *happiness*. To try to culture happiness may seem to destroy that elusive mood. There are those who will always feel that anguish and ecstasy and suffering and bliss must be allowed to take their spontaneous place in the nature of human existence – as un-programmed as thunder and lightening and as fleeting as a rainbow. There are those who will feel that any attempt to capture happiness must have the same effect as forgoing the beauty of the wild flowers by the wayside in favour of formal gardens.

This is a romantic idiom, which has much merit and should never be discarded. Romance is made for dreams and dreams are an essential ingredient of happiness. But the *laissez-faire* attitude to happiness is too wasteful, too negligent and too selfish. Very few people ever have the chance to enjoy except for brief moments the spontaneous happiness of the roadside wild flowers. And in any case that is not being abandoned. Today, flowers by the wayside will only be preserved if we make a deliberate effort to preserve them. The world has become complex and the pressures are great and confusing. They do not disappear because a few people can remove themselves to still lyrical parts of the countryside. Most people have to cope with a world, which they might wish to be simpler and more lyrical, but without an effort on their part the world will not spontaneously move in this direction.

Townspeople often show a disregard for nature or at least a lack of appreciation. Country people feel that sensitivity to nature needs to be developed by attention and exposure. In the same way a sensitivity to happiness needs to be developed by attention and exposure.

All things wise and wonderful
The Lord God makes them all
Each little flower that opens,
Each little bird that sings,
God made their glowing colours,
And made their tiny wings.

Hymn

chapter 5

Health & Beauty

 **TIP**

Many of us don't realise how special we are.
We all DESERVE to be TRULY LOVED and to choose a
HAPPY STATE for ourselves.
We are all BEAUTIFUL INSIDE and OUT.

SHELLEY SYKES
THE HAPPINESS GURU

Have you ever noticed that some people look good ALL the time, even when they are feeling sick and others, they can look sick when actually they are feeling well?

Part of being happy and contaminated by **The Happiness Bug** is to look and feel great all the time. Not a bad symptom to have if you're currently one of the ones that look sick when you are healthy!

I must tell you that one of the most alluring and beautiful parts of a person are their eyes. It is said they are the 'windows to the soul.' The eyes themselves never look any older they always seem to have that same colour and sparkle whether a person is 8 or 80 years young.

We are all beautiful inside and out, but as we all know that dehydrated skin with funny looking hairs poking out does not look as attractive as smooth, well-maintained plumped out skin. Like a palace, if well maintained it can look new and inviting and the treasures inside a lure, but if left un-maintained it can look much much older, decrepit, smelly and very uninviting. I know that I would prefer to be that well maintained palace.

Some as we have just said have a natural talent and even a passion about enjoying good health, clothes, style, looking and feeling great.
The good news is that this is a learnable skill. I am dedicating a whole chapter to this area in our lives because having been involved in the health and beauty industry for the past 17 years I really KNOW how it affects peoples self-esteem and quality of life.

It's no good looking gorgeous and having no energy, equally its no good looking and feeling less than best. So for those of you who naturally 'get it' and are looking and feeling great this chapter will just be revision, although I have placed some very new and key points that might just give you the edge!
I will spend this time focused on those of you, who really need some help with your health and image.
Like any big break-through it is always the simple things that take us to the next stage. You don't have to be super determined, have will power or a big bank balance to look and feel healthy and happy.

According to David Meyers a leading positive psychologist, happy people tend to have 4 main characteristics:

- High self-esteem
- Optimistic
- Out-going personality
- Feeling of control over life

So in this chapter we are going to apply this research to the way we now think and feel particularly in respect to **'feeling that we have control over our life'** in fact we are going to be optimistic and state that we know that we can control:

- What we eat
- How fit we become
- How deep and well we breath
- How often we exercise
- How we stand and walk
- How we groom ourselves.

Many of us have seen the 'Biggest Loser' weight loss reality TV show. The contestants are beautiful people in the most abused bodies. We know that they have given up their control.

The three main reasons that they say they are over weight is:

- They put more food in their mouths than they burn up.
- It is a habit and the thought association of self-love.
- Hiding themselves subconsciously believing they are not enough.

We all give up a little control if we are even slightly over weight or not as fit as we know we can be. The good news is, that we can all take control back right now, just like the biggest losers do on TV.

I think we can all agree that if the biggest losers can change their thinking and habits we can. It is possible.
Dr Tickle has proven after a 90-day program that anyone can look and be 10 times fitter, stronger and thinner just taking small steps in the right direction. At the Forever Young Clinics we have had the most amazing results in weight reduction, energy and vitality increase not to mention cellulite and wrinkle reduction. It's great isn't it!

I told you that the solution to health and beauty is going to be simple.
'*Think Thin and Breath Better*' – the name of one of my books.

Thinking

1. It is proven that our analytical brain controls all our bodily functions. We can control our breathing, it is even possible to control our metabolic rate, blood pressure, heart-beat if we re learn the techniques that some of the monks still exercise, but most time our brain takes over and does it for us.

    It has been said that what we think we become.
    Well start thinking, fit, slim and beautiful every day. It really works. Our brain never wants to be wrong so it starts providing you with the matching body form. Slim, fit, healthy, beautiful and well.

2. The Meta Physicians have proven that our water filled bodies are sensitive to thought patterning. Dr Masaru Emoto of IHM General Research Institute in Japan has proven that water after being blessed, then frozen, crystallises differently depending on the naming. Water blessed and named 'love' has beautiful crystals, named 'hate' the water crystallises into sharp jagged shards, when viewed under a microscope.

3. Have you noticed grouchy people are often sickly people and don't live that long?
    Be happy and live longer. Think beautiful healthy slim fit thoughts!

Breathing

1. It is a proven fact that deep diagrammatic breathing **increases the lymphatic system 16 times.** Our lymph carries our toxins and excreta around our bodies from our cells. Some people are like walking sewerage tanks! By breathing much deeper and exhaling hard 6 times a day you can speed up the flow of lymph, since it doesn't have a pump. The lungs work almost like a pump to get the lymph moving so that our cells in our bodies don't end up bathing in it's own yuck and die. Remember that most cancers are morphed cells triggered by toxins, poisons, and negative thoughts.

2. Our cells and body stays looking younger and fresher. All cells need oxygen. Breath deeply if you want **to look younger!**

3. The third benefit of course is that the deep breathing gives us more oxygen, which results in **more Energy** to do all those things that we find fun.

4. You **lose weight** over night just by deep diagrammatic breathing, because you end up weeing more and getting rid of the toxins. Drinking water really helps too.

Water

1. I have had a saying for years 'Water in – Weight off!' If you drink 8 x 600mls of water a day then you certainly start losing all those extra pounds and help flush out toxic fluids.

2. Bowels, stomach, kidneys and liver stay in good condition as does the skin and the brain. Don Tollman – the Indiana Jones of Health says that we should drink water – the 'weight of our brains,' so that we keep all the functions in our bodies in balance and our brain at optimum function.

3. **No more headaches** and you stay bright and alert. Concentration really improves and you literally stay turgid like a well-watered plant, rather than limp, listless and dehydrated. Turgid asparagus stems rather than limp and listless or a plump peach rather than a dried out prune? So drink lots of WATER. 'Happy Love Mineral Water' is packed with high vibrational crystal energy.' Check out the website www.happywater.com

Physical Fitness

Walking reduces stress and alleviates anger.

Walking tightens bottom muscles and increases ones metabolic rate to burn fat.

Walking up steps reduces fat, improves muscle tone and improves circulation.

By increasing our physical activity we stimulate the body to produce endorphins, which are **natural opiates** – the bodies natural happiness drug!

When we exercise regularly we feel better, look better and we are better. Feeling stronger with higher self-esteem and all those endorphins, why wouldn't you want to exercise? With MP3 players these days playing your favourite music the time just swings by and you can really put your body and soul into the movement.

If you really don't feel like walking or the gym is just not you, then try 'Sexercise'. This type of exercise is excellent for those of you, who are serious about getting flat tummies and tight bottoms and want to increase all your endorphins for a much better skin complexion and youthful look.

Many of my female clients that had 'gone off sex' have dived back into it with vigour to get their womanly shapes back – and their husbands are thrilled to be 'used' in their wives physical workout program. It's certainly increased their connection, passion levels and communication as a couple. As the lady gets to look better, her self-esteem returns and she starts to be a lot flirtier and cheekier. It's fun having a great body!

There are other ways of losing inches; I personally think the physical effort or the machines that physically break down cellulite, which we use at Forever Young, are far more effective than the injections that are invasive. It's even better long term than liposuction, because these latter two create waves of fat afterwards if people put on any more weight and they look worse than with just the cellulite that was the initial problem. Do take advice before doing anything invasive that can have long-term effects. Seeing people's bodies afterwards is a sure way to give anyone doubts.

Skin Care

Now for all of you who are still using soap and water for your faces – I suggest you keep up with the times! The reason we use cleansers and toners is to save our skin working 39 minutes longer per day, versus 1 minute, when we use a cleanser to clean the skin and toner to remove any cleanser. Soap cleans the skin, but it removes all the natural oils and dries it out so the skin has to work hard for 20 minutes to rebalance it's self. Washing twice a day for example has our skin working for 40 minutes with soap versus 30 seconds each time with cleansers and toners. By reducing the working time of our skin by 39 mins per day x 7 days per week x 52 weeks in a year, it makes sense if we don't work our skin too hard that we appear younger or look younger for longer.

There will be those that say 'oh well, I don't use soap or cleansers I just splash with water.' This is equally destructive to your skin cells, because every night we excrete uric acid onto our faces (pooh) and that needs to be washed off with something stronger than just gorgeous water. When you wake up and kiss your partner before getting up and cleansing your faces ... you are actually kissing one another's pooh!

Anti-Aging is the next trillion-dollar industry according to the futurists and Harvard business economists. We know that the **power of feeling good** about ourselves results in **higher self-esteem** and increased **energy** to take more action and do more things in life.

Depressed people or people with low self-esteem do far less in their day than someone happy and energised.

Extreme **surgery** has become rife, but I must let you know there are new technological ways that help you remain younger looking for longer, combined with a consistent home routine, that really does work and is non-invasive.

It goes without saying that stress and holes in the ozone layer cause our skins to dehydrate and blemish much more quickly. It is very important that **we all moisturise**. The issue is with so many cosmetic companies out there stating their products have xyz ingredients that help reduce lines and keep skin plumped, it is hard determining, which products actually have enough of that special ingredient that actually makes a difference.

It used to be easy when you could go on price, but now even the most expensive products don't mean that their concentration and potency is any better. Often the price reflects more the costs of the packaging and the marketing campaign and point of sale (department store floor space is exorbitantly expensive, the models for the adverts, commercials and R & D all are costed out in to each of those little jars).

There are a few of us that really campaign for and research the products that really do make a difference. Listen I want to look younger myself for longer – so why not have a piece of the trillion dollar industry and look great too. Having Anti-Aging and Allergy Clinics really helps, because we have the resources to test out the products and see the differences! (Check out www.foreveryoungclinics.com).

With modern technology creams have come along way. Creams with high does of vitamin C and other minerals certainly stimulate ADP and ATP molecules (elastin and collagen) to plump out fine lines and reduce the signs of sun damage and melanin markings. A great cream will also have high doses of humectants to plump and acids to help reduce the layers of dead skin on the surface so that the serums and creams can do their magic.

Although the **real magic is done by machines** – which shorten and thicken the muscles, that have begun to droop with wear and tear and the pull of gravity. Many of us have seen people, who have had Bels Palsy or strokes where the face muscles have been affected and have dropped dramatically on one side of the face. The people look out of balance and of course their self-esteem drops. The medical profession devised a machine to shorten and thicken the muscles and put them back into place. It worked! It worked better than they ever imagined, because this same machine that put muscles back into place also stimulated these ADP and ATP molecules and plumped out the patient's lines around their eyes and mouths, they lost their double chins and crêpe necks!

The machines are in the next stages of development. **Forever Young** wanted to keep abreast of the technology in order to get the best results for each client.

These **machines**, in combination with **potent creams** used at home, result in glowing, plumped out, youthful skin that is firm and kissable! It is a team effort. At Forever Young we devised a way to give the optimum skin treatments in one go and developed the 4-in-1 Facial. Instead of having to choose one of 4 possible treatments, all great in their own right, we combined the whole lot and charge as if for 1 treatment. The results are amazing skin for men, women and even those with severe blemishes and the clinics are busy. People fly in from different states and from overseas to have these treatments at the Forever Young Clinics.

I know some of you will be screaming out – 'what do you think to the 'injections', Botox, Restalin, Aqualine?' Whilst some of you are cringing and going 'oh no!'

These Injections are big business for many doctors. I personally have seen people with lumps where before they had fine lines and crevices and the lumps look worse.

I think **frown marks** or scowls can make people look very angry or moody, not good if you really are a bubbly bright happy person. Since the Forever Young 4-in-1 anti-aging facial machines contract muscle and frowns are very contracted muscle, the machines cannot get rid of the frown marks. Botox certainly can relax the muscle and stop the muscle contracting and some filler helps plump out the crease. The result is very noticeable and in some cases well worth the discomfort.

We have all heard the jokes about Botox taking away your smile around the mouth, drooping eyelids and hearing of ladies that can hardly blink – well watch out, this can happen. I personally think many people have too much Botox applied around their faces and personally I think they look expressionless and so they become in my opinion less attractive. In the effort to looking healthier and younger we still need to keep the balance and our power of attraction displaying our personality and character.

Personally I do believe in having unsightly moles or big marks removed, because they detract people's attention from your eyes and smile. Moles can also grow into malformed cells, so it is always a good thing in my opinion to have them removed even if it is for peace of mind. Here in Australia there are nearly as many skin cancer clinics as there are beauty salons, so be aware.

Remember though, that we are all beautiful in our own unique ways and having expression lines and showing our emotion on our faces is very alluring and magnetic.

So please use your own discretion. If a physical change will help boost your self-esteem and it's going to be a benefit then do something about it, after weighing up all the benefits, the pros and the cons. I think you are beautiful anyway!

Hair

Hair can be our crowning glory, that's if we have it. Guys I can sympathise with those of you, who have lost or are losing it. I had my hair burnt off my head once by a hair salon and it was one of the worst experiences of my life. Waking up in a morning with hair laying on my pillow after I got up, or washing the remnants of my hair in the shower and chunks remaining entwined around my fingers! It's nightmare stuff unless you see the positive. Men that lose their hair have high male hormones and high stamina. Many women love men with shaved heads – they think it is cool and I bet they like the high male testosterone levels too!

For those of you with hair, take heed of your head. Your hair frames your face and there is nothing nicer than a good haircut and shiny hair.

Hygiene is paramount to increasing your energy and vibration. So guys, I suggest you don't stick more gel on your head instead of washing it – it will still smell and girls don't just stick it in a crunchy, when it really needs a wash – wash it. The bounce and the shine will empower you for the day and there is nothing sexier for a guy than a girl with swishy hair – just look at all those hair shampoo and hair colour adverts – All the girls swish their hair!

Both men and women use colour in their hair these days. It's great, because it can boost your vibrant personality. **Colour** adds texture, depth and vibrancy. It also allows you to have a change. A summer look, versus a winter look can be sassy or sophisticated. Once again it is down to choice and your personality.

I had to laugh, when I once did a survey on women's hairstyles. I kept hearing the comment from men that they preferred girls with long hair, BUT the comment was that many women cut it off as soon as they got married. It seemed a very general statement to make yet the results from the research showed that within one year of marriage many women had their long locks cut off. When we asked these ladies why – they said it was for convenience. It was easier and quicker to manage short, cropped hair. Yet asked why they had kept it long for so long before they surprised themselves by saying 'my boyfriend liked me with long hair'. When asked if they felt sexier with short hair or long hair, they surprisingly said they felt sexier with longer hair.
So what does this tell us?

Even though we are a modern society and even though we know to do things for ourselves and not for others, once we find our men, ladies don't give up so quickly on being the feminine, attractive girls just for convenience. Divorce is now at it's highest of 50%.
Groom yourself as if still 'Sexy and Single', even when married, because it maintains your own confidence levels, sex appeal and attraction levels.

With **The Happiness Bug** you can focus and enjoy what you have. Most people become unhappy when they have curly hair and want it straight or straight haired people want their hair to have body, bounce and curl. Red heads want black shiny hair, black haired people love blondes, in fact all colours want to have blonde at least for a short while and natural blondes don't know what the fuss is all about.

If we can look after and **appreciate our own qualities** we will have more joy and happiness.
I can now tell you the gratitude I have that I actually have hair and that it has grown back. Do I condition my hair daily, yes absolutely? Do I use organic colours to be gentler, yes you bet! Do I have a professional cut regularly, with out doubt. Is my hair my crowning glory – yes! Thanks Roberto!

Appreciate what you have, wether it is a lot or not, thick or thin, curly or straight, long or short. Make a decision to go with the flow and utilise the best characteristics you have to match the look you want to have for your personality. There are no mistakes in nature. My son Rory (means Red King) has golden red hair and has the personality to match, fiery and bright.

Teeth and Nails

If you thought I made a big issue about hair and skin, 'teeth' are my thing.
Our smiles are one of the most enigmatic ways for communicating with others. A smiley person definitely attracts more people and has more friends than those that don't. Why? Because it is showing the other person that you are interested in them and are open to connect.

Dale Carnegie said that, "You can make more friends in two months by becoming interested in other people than you can in two years by trying to get other people interested in you."

I love smiling and I make sure my teeth are in great condition. My dentist, Sam is one of my best friends now along with my hairdresser. I want the best and travel to have experts work on one of my best assets, my teeth.

The Americans are definitely far more conscious of good teeth than many other countries, because they realised years ago, the power of the smile.

 **TIP**

Make sure you have a bright white smile and good breath. You'll have a lot more friends and feel happier!

SHELLEY SYKES
THE HAPPINESS GURU

We all have had bad breath at some stage during the week. Perhaps it is, because we haven't eaten regularly, bacteria builds up on the tongue or it could be that spicy meal we had the night before. I carry a toothbrush in the car, at the office and of course at home. People will move closer if you have great breath and step back if you haven't – watch out for the signs.

Clothes

It has been proven that by dressing up we actually feel more empowered. Don't you just love it, when you are freshly showered and you put on new underwear and then your new clothes and new shoes? You actually feel new and energised. It feels great to know everything looks good on every level...

Putting the same new clothes on with old underwear just doesn't feel the same. Or putting on new shoes with old socks takes away from the splendour of having 'nice stuff' on all the levels. No one else can tell looking at you that you have old underwear or old socks on, but YOU KNOW and it changes the feeling.

Now this **doesn't** mean that you need to go out shopping every week for new stuff – no. What it does mean is that what we want to do is **create that great feeling every time** you put on clothes. Your clothes have to look, feel and mean something special to you for your own dignity and self-esteem.

Certain items in your wardrobe when you put them on make you feel 'great' no matter how long you have had them. These type of outfits; are the sort that should be filling your wardrobe and that you should be wearing on a daily basis. As a stylist to the stars and many thousands of clients around the world for many years one of my jobs was to find clothes and styles that suited my clients:

- Lifestyle
- Personality
- Mood and
- The Occasion.

Each outfit had to fit into all 4 criteria's to be congruent with their persona that they were creating or had created. All the presidents and their wives have to become styled for their new roles as head of governments. Pop stars are continually reinventing themselves to match and mirror or reflect their new music. It's no good singing like Mary Poppins and dressing like a Hells Angel (although this Modern Day Mary Poppins sing-alike, dresses like a pink rapper for the single *'I'm the Rappin Mama'*!). Corporate businessmen dress differently to those working in a holiday resort.

For example a successful business man that travels a lot with his work and is taken out for meals by clients, attends gala dinners, yet when at home goes sailing on his boat and enjoys relaxing and socialising with his social bubbly wife and their kids will have probably:

- Dinner suit and matching accessories with several cummerbunds
- 6 × great suits varying in colours from Navy to Cream.
- Strong bright ties with some coloured shirts to match his suits and ties.
- 8 × pairs of shoes, 3 pairs x black, brown, navy, cream, boating loafers, moccasins with matching belts.
- 3 × Sailor type sweater and matching shorts
- 3 × swimmer shorts and T shirts
- 4 pairs of casual smart tailored trousers
- 2 × pairs jeans
- 5 × stylish casual shirts
- 2 × silk knit fine jumpers
- 3 × stylish T shirts
- 3 × ¾ cropped casual trousers
- 1 × leather jacket
- 1 × casual cashmere jacket
- 1 × over coat long
- 1 × rain jacket short

This man will be fitted out now ready for any type of occasion that suits his life. The colour of ties and shirts show and reflect his personality. The quality and cut of his suits defines this man with high self-esteem.

His foot-ware (and women check shoes guys), match his different styles of clothing, whether smart or casual.

Even his casual is trendy, but stylish.

The words here are 'appropriate'.

Business ladies are similar, but they can mix in their wardrobes dresses that are stylishly cut with colour for work that can be blended with jackets and mixed with colour and of course the selection of shoe styles, heights of heel and colours can be far more varied. Women are lucky too, that the selection of eveningwear can be so glamorous yet come in different styles and lengths from long to cocktail, to clingy and short or evening trouser suits . . .

A mum with 2 kids can still have an exciting wardrobe. You don't have to have the token 'trakki' (tracksuit) with baggy bottom and bulging knees.

Shoes and Accessories

We have just mentioned **shoes** and these are so important to an outfits overall appearance, besides the practicality of them. There are some fabulous styles for both men and women these days. The cut and shape, softness of the leather and design of stitch allow shoes to be more fun and glamorous.

Ideally shoes should be the same colour as the trouser hem or the hemline of the skirt. If you were wearing navy trousers then ideally navy shoes and navy belt would be the most appropriate.

If you are wearing a pink skirt then ideally the shoes or the sandals should be the same colour as the skirt, pink and NOT the colour of the top, as many women mistakenly try to match up.

Handbags often let the woman down. Many women have beautiful clothes and matching shoes and then grab 'their big ol' bag' full of their 'bits' and it won't even match the outfit, shoes or anything often dragged along with them like a well worn loved teddy bear.

If I can give you any advice ladies let this be it – Change your handbags to match your outfits...every day. Just place what you need in your bag and nothing more!

It is true that the accessories make an outfit. You can have cheaper garments, but if you have quality shoes, clean and colour co-ordinated the outfit looks so much more expensive and tailored. Matching belts and matching bags are also key.

I express over and over to clients not to just get a bag and belt, because of its colour match, but instead to chose a belt or bag that you really like, since they are expensive investment items and need to be enjoyed.

Other accessories such as **jewellery**, watches and pens even should be picked because you like them and they suit your personality and style. I have a girl friend in South Africa, Amanda who has; over the years collected watches and now has a different watch for every outfit. Each watch was picked for it's own style and beauty. Some are more expensive than others. All the watches make her feel special. Often they are conversational pieces. I, on the other hand, have just one watch I wear for evening and for daytime. It took me awhile to save up for it, but I really like the style design and it suits my personality. I never feel too much 'sparkle' is too much!

There are those who like to wear all their 'bling-bling' in one go, like the modern day Hip Hop Rappers. It is their style. It's not for me personally. I like to go for the more simple and sophisticated look.

I do however recommend if people are going to wear accessories that they are clean. Many ladies particularly wear rings that get layered with creams and grease – gunge that dulls the sparkle of diamonds and starts to go black in the creases of the gold.

The cheapest, most effective and easiest way to clean jewellery is with washing-up liquid or shampoo and an old toothbrush. It brings gold and diamonds or other stones back to full shine and sparkle! The alternative is to have your jewellery sonically cleaned at the jewellers.

Even the **briefcase, pen, wallet** you use reflects your personality and image.

NB. According to some of the Feng Shui philosophers, green purses or wallets attract more wealth in! So yes, I have a green purse.

Make-up

Make-up has been used down the centuries to enhance a persons features particularly the eyes. Cleopatra was certainly one that promoted make-up so that she could hide the lines around her eyes. Her aim was to look, young and fresh like a younger woman.

Make-up certainly helps. It has been assessed through various university studies that ladies wearing make-up actually get **promoted quicker** and **earn 30% more** than their counterparts that are 'au naturel'! So what does that say to us? Ladies start wearing make-up if you want to be promoted and earn more! It also means that managers see women workers, who apply make-up and take particular attention to their appearance, assume that they must have higher self-esteem and will be more capable of looking after business and their clients!

Think about it, if a person can't be bothered to put their 'face on' in the morning, they are more likely, not to be bothered about others too. Some one who pays attention to them-selves will most likely pay attention to others!

Men, facial grooming is also important. Attention to nose hair and eyebrows is important. Clean-shaven men definitely are seen to be more trustworthy and caring. Again it is down to perceptions of taking time for themselves and then for others. Men really aught to have monthly facials to clean out the blocked pores on their skin such as the Forever Young 4-in-1 industrial facial. Even the muscle tightening treatment is worth considering keeping the 'Peter Pan' looks in tact.

Remember the more we love ourselves and take care the more we will attract love and attention from others.

Edward de Bono's comments

There is a notion that there is a divide between thinking on one hand and beauty and feeling on the other. It is sometimes believed that thinking destroys spontaneous emotional response and also kills beauty by analysis. It is imagined that the thinking person stands in front of a painting and instead of appreciating its beauty and responding with an emotion, analyses the style of the painter. This is a silly misconception fostered by those who equate thinking with intellectual games. The appreciation of beauty and feeling itself are types of thinking. The only difference is that they are not carried out with words or fixed concepts. To be able to feel about something is as important as, or even more important than, being able to think about it. But feelings should not exclude other forms of thinking since each can enhance the other. The new happy system in no way suggests that everything has to be reduced to intellectual formulas. Thinking in the ordinary sense of the word, is only a tool of feeling. Shelley emphasises the value of feeling good and the benefits that that result in. The tool is used to create those situations in which enjoyment and happiness can best be felt.

There is a classical story of the centipede that was proceeding quite comfortably until someone asked it which leg followed which. The result was that the centipede became unable to proceed further as it lay distracted in the ditch wondering which leg came before which. There are those who feel that thinking will destroy their ability to feel or appreciate in an unintellectual way. Again it must be stressed that there is a big difference between thinking and intellectual analysis. Thinking enlarges the area in which feeling can take place and generates more opportunities for feeling: there is no antagonism between the two. A person who looks brilliantly by 'instinct' is not made to follow an instruction book, but benefits from being brought into contact with new ingredients to which he can apply skill.

chapter 6

Wealth & Worry

 **TIP**

There is never a wrong moment or never a right moment…
All moments are just great.

SHELLEY SYKES
THE HAPPINESS GURU

It is true that our modern pace of life is 200 times faster than it was 10 years ago and this speed of life is accelerating, because of our ability to communicate faster and smarter with the help of the Internet and satellite communications just to name two.

What I had to learn at University level is being taught to kindergarten kids, who are now growing up with computers and interactive TV in their homes and classrooms.

With so much information traveling through the ether and so much for our wonderful brains to process we have to be able to decipher quicker and smarter. **It is expected that we make decisions more quickly and to act and do more in the 24 hours. It's what we all have each day.**

Good organisers can leverage from this fast flow. Many people become wealthy, because of it. More access to customers through the Internet, quicker solutions, faster delivery times, more products available to sell, people to service . . .

These people use leverage and add value to what they do to create wealth. They stay focused and manage their time well. They feel the fear, but do it anyway.

For many people this constant bombardment of information and pressure to act can be overwhelming. It can be scary, because jobs postponed can soon become mountainous. Emails are a great example. Emailing is one of the best quickest ways to communicate at any time of day or night to anywhere in the world, cheaply and quickly without being intrusive, because people can pick up messages at their convenience. I really appreciate having the Internet and being able to communicate with friends and clients any time, anywhere for any reason. Leave them a day or two especially if you are a busy communicator like me and they mount up so that it can take 'hours' to respond and it can become unbearable . . .

 **TIP**

General life can feel like an 'in-box' full of emails for many people – Just too many to handle. An over load!

SHELLEY SYKES
THE HAPPINESS GURU

Teenage suicide is the highest it has ever been, yet our kids today have more than any other generation in education, material wealth, gadgets, opportunities to travel, communication options, a voice to be heard and freedoms of expression. Depression amongst both men and women has doubled in the past 5 years alone. Despite the ease of life with modern technology such as washing machines, mobiles, computers, DVD's, cars and planes, which cut down time that in the past took people to do, expectations have risen to do MORE and can contribute to worry. This overload needs to be handled.

Worry is the biggest killer of ENERGY and the instigator of most ailments from allergy to cancerous growths. **Worry is being anxious about the future, about things that may never happen, about what could be.** It is the most negative of feelings and leads to procrastination, depression, premature aging, sickness and lethargy. Why do something if...?

False Myths – In the modern world we have been taught that it is prudent to worry. We have been taught that to prepare for the worst is smart... It is even thought of as a caring trait to have if you 'worry about your children'.

The Happiness Bug zaps worry. **Those people with The Happiness Bug feel the fear, but do it anyway!**

They know that worry will suck away their energies and affect their sleep, they know that it can make them sick, so they assume the best result NOT the worst and if anything bad happens they just handle it if and when it happens. It is always less horrific when you are dealing with a bad situation than it is 'thinking' it.

My mum is a prime example of worry. She worries about me and my son living in Australia on our own, she worries about my sister, she worries about what is going on in Iraq, because that will affect interest rates in the UK if they send soldiers and then all the mortgage interest rates will increase ... then how will she manage to live on her pension?

I received a call from her best friend in Spain saying mum had been taken in to hospital. It was a shock, because mum despite being a worrier had always been healthy and was only in her early 60's.
I was ready to get on the next plane, but Moyra her friend said no ... don't she is just having tests, because of the pains she had had.

For a whole week, all forms of possibilities occurred to me. I began to worry ... what if ... I started to cry at inappropriate times, not sleep and generally look tired and ill myself. I felt 'out of control' and useless. It was funny to hear later that at that same time Mums friends suddenly became doctors and she was being diagnosed by friends ... oh its Diabetes, Wind, Bowels, Broken ribs ... You have to laugh!

I came to the conclusion that I was **being silly worrying** about what it could be and that **I had to trust** that she was in the best place with the best qualified and know I would know if there was anything serious. I knew this was a testing time for **The Happiness Guru** to prove that **The Happiness Bug** still remained infected even in stressful situations. I had several days of relief just trusting. Knowing at this time I was better to keep my strength up and keep positive for my son, my clients and my mum as well as myself.

Finally the tests came through and Moyra phoned. Mum had been diagnosed with a malignant 6cm cancerous tumor in her uterus! The specialist surgeon had been booked and the doctors were to operate almost straight away. The shock was still horrific and yes of course I cried, but I took action and this took away a lot of the pain and 'worry'.

I booked a flight to Spain, cancelled all my appointments, organised friends to look after my son and jumped on a plane. All the worrying was for nothing. It had made no difference to the outcome. Luckily, I had had a few days of peace and built up my energies. Taking action was a relief and being with mum in hospital was far less painful than 'thinking about the possibilities of cancer and death'.

All the worrying in the world would not make the cancer go away. Being happy and strong was a benefit, because I was able to support and stay 15 hours a day in the hospital by her side. I did suffer jet lag and kindly her friend came and gave me a break on a couple occasions. I relished those times so that I could go back renewed. Better that, then refusing help and 'worrying' or becoming overly tired and then no use to mum.

Seeing mum get a little stronger each day was a bonus. I was able to 'do' things for her and keep her company. We were able to talk and I was able to speak some Spanish and build a report with the nursing staff and the Spanish lady in the next bed, to make mum's stay in hospital less scary. Seeing mum in pain and struggling with the whole situation was painful, but I handled it. I was able to manage my emotions too. Seeing me upset only upset mum. We all just had to remain calm and tranquil and go with the flow.

As I repeatedly say 'shit happens' in everyone's life. Happiness is not about rapping yourself up in cotton wool, nor is it about controlling as many situations as you can – No. It is about handling all life's circumstances and looking for the lesson and the new doors that open because of the situation. It isn't what happens to you in life that counts, but what we do about it that matters.

When the 'bad things happen' it brings us back into appreciation mode. We can remember to be grateful about all the good that is happening.

So you might say what good came out of mum having cancer . . . well there were many things I came up with.

1. Mum had a flood of well wishes and cards from around the world acknowledging their love and respect of her. (Sometimes living alone one never truly appreciates how much people do care and love us.)
2. Her friends and neighbors came to the rescue and rallied around contacting friends and family, visiting her in hospital in shifts, bringing her food and clothes and bits and bobs into the hospital, feeding her cat and checking on the house. They were and still are great.
3. She had me jetting around the world to sit by her side and keep vigil through love and not duty. We appreciated each other's time together and our love shone and energised us both.
4. It brought my wayward sister back into the fold . . . and despite the terrible things she had done to mum, the time had come to put that aside and for her to offer support to mum in mum's time of need.

5. Her determination to get well and enjoy life and good health from now on was evident. A turning point for her to truly appreciate all the good that is happening in her life.

Focusing on the good keeps us happy, enjoying the adventure of life keeps us growing and moving forward. We can then live in the present and look forward to the future rather than 'WORRY' about the future.

A great mantra for the people that 'used to worry' can be:

Life is good and all is well.

The Happiness Bug Secret to overcome Worry

- The secret is NOT to WORRY – focus on the good things and the new doors that are opening not the ones that have just closed.
- Trust that all will be well.
- Take action when it is needed.
- Trust that every moment is just perfect as it is.
- What ever you do is just enough.

Wealth

One of the biggest causes for worry is the lack of money or not enough to live on in the manor you would like. But is wealth how much money you have?

I asked many of the financial whizzes what their definition of wealth was and Roger Hamilton from the XL Results Foundation summed it up beautifully as:

Wealth = Value × Leverage

Basically, **wealth is what you have left when there is no more money left.**

Think about it. Wealth is what you have left when all the money is taken out of the equation.

- Its your ideas
- Your health
- Your family
- Your contacts
- Your relationships
- Your friends
- Its your beliefs and faith
- Its your self-esteem and confidence
- Its your humor and joy
- Your love of life
- Your compassion
- Your Dreams

Wow, I realised I am one of the wealthiest people alive!! Just like you too probably! In the western world most of us are WEALTHY and don't know it.

But if you are like me at this moment in time I am wealthy with a bank balance that could be much healthier! I am lucky, because I have in the past made money and so know it is possible, but I have also lost money, which can be a concern.

I asked the experts, people with millions and billions on their asset listings what makes the difference between 'wealthy' people with little money and 'wealthy' people with loads of money!

Surprisingly, they like me had all made loads, but lost loads before they got the answer to my question and they said the answer was 'LUCK' as we mentioned before.

L – Location
U – Understanding
C – Connections & Contacts
K – Knowledge

Richard Branson agrees with this verdict, **Donald Trump** agrees too. When Donald lost his fortune it wasn't long before he made it back and more. How? He had ideas and the determination and persistence to make it happen. He had contacts; people with money and people with knowledge that could team up and leverage his plans into action. Plus he chose his location well.

Remember:

Wealth = Value x Leverage

John Paul Getty valued his time as the ideas man, the man with connections working 'on' his business not in it and allowing others to make these ideas a reality. Just like **Walt Disney** . . . such big ideas, but he alone could not have done it single handedly. He needed to enroll an investor that could also 'see' the possibility of his dream and a team of knowledgeable people to make it happen. We all know his dream has come true – Disney World and all the movies is a worldwide organisation that touches the lives of young and old alike. It is fun and magical just as Disney had hoped and knew it could be and would be. He persisted with his dream until it became a reality. Just like **Sylvester Stallone** with his movie idea 'Rocky'. He and his script were rejected by over 100 movie-producers. The one or two that seemed keen didn't want him playing in the movie. He stood his ground. His dream was to be 'Rocky' and he knew it was going to be a hit despite what the producers and critics were saying. Rocky I had the best return on investment and a best-selling film...the rest is history with Rocky II and Rocky III being huge hits and Sylvester being turned into a super star.

We can all be financially free if we trust ourselves and have faith in our own dreams and ideas. We need to choose our location well, build a team and find willing investors. If our idea is a force for good or benefits many the likelihood that the rewards will be great are increased.

With every wealthy, financially free person I have had the privilege to meet he or she all had one thing in common and that besides being lucky was PASSION. They had all been passionate about their dream or ideas. **Branson** was passionate about music and Virgin records was created. He didn't plan from the beginning to make billions and own empires in travel, make-up, banking, and ballooning... **Donald Trump** is passionate about wheeling and dealing. He loves the challenge and never envisaged perhaps being a TV personality as well as a property magnet. **Walt Disney** didn't create Disney World to make billions, but it does. Just like footballers and Internet magnets didn't set out to make billions... they just did and do what they are passionate about and be their best. It is then during this time of being in the flow that creates the wealth for themselves and others. **Roger Hamilton** is passionate about worldwide wealth. He passionately believes that it is possible to get rid of poverty in our lifetime, if we the wealthy share the knowledge and secret of wealth creation and the belief in abundance. There is enough for us all. According to some of the economists there is $13 trillion dollars a day flying around the world!

If however we have a poverty mentality instead of coming from the belief we are 'all' wealthy we somehow attract more poverty and hardships.

Rowland and Flora's story

Just before I flew to Spain I was invited to meet a very special man and one of his fellow country ladies from Malawi at a fund raising awareness meeting in Sydney. This man, Rowland had a dream to help his people gain self-esteem and confidence to create their own wealth and food stocks instead of accepting handouts from the worldwide charity organisations each year when the dry season hit and the food was in short supply.

Flora was a local Malawi woman, a typical woman in her village living in a one-roomed house with a husband that hit her when stressed over money. His rule was absolute, over his wife and two children. They felt that their life was their life and could not envisage it ever improving. She was illiterate and even though she had a dream to own and live in a 4-roomed house she felt it was an impossibility.

When Rowland arrived in her village with the Worldwide Food Organisation saying that 'they could help each person improve their lot'... Flora and her husband didn't believe them. She just wanted the free charitable handouts that she was now used to getting.

Rowland and the World Food campaigners didn't give up. They held free meetings in the village square and asked the villages questions that they themselves had not even thought about. Why could other people at the other side of the world have so much food that they could give them their spare food? The villagers said 'it was God's will'. So Rowland asked them the question 'what do 'these people overseas' do that is so special that God would allow them to have more than his loving and faithful people in Africa?'

Rowland wrote on a board, 'Africans' on one side and 'Foreigners' on the other. He said well the Foreigners have 2 arms and 2 legs just like the Africans, they have land to plant food like the Africans, they can't control the weather just like the Africans so they use their skill to build irrigations systems... this was possible in Africa. The Foreigners help one another and group their resources, which the Africans can also do...

It dawned on the villagers that they weren't that different from these 'unknown peoples', who supplied them with their excess food. It was encouraging to know that they had all the basics to generate their own wealth. Many of the women volunteered to be trained by the World Food Organisation. Flora was one of them. The WFO set about building a base which supported a doctor and midwife, a mini bank to help the women get started, a store room and shop where goods and services could be exchanged or bartered.

Flora borrowed money to buy three pigs and some extra money to plant some food for the pigs to eat on her little plot.

Her pigs flourished. They produced 20 piglets and she kept, 6 and sold 14 paying off some of the debt. She paid for her children to go to school and have enough money to buy food for 3 meals a day.

Her next litter of piglets produced 42 and once again she sold many to pay off the debt so some other lady could borrow money and start her own business. She also had enough cash to buy land and build a 4-roomed house on it. She had enough money for clothes and money left to loan to other women, so that she could give back to her community and show them it was possible.

Now her husband doesn't hit her. Their finance problems are over and she has an equal say in the household, she earned his respect and built up her own self-esteem.

Other villagers planted seeds and kept much of the good harvest in store along with the other farmers so that when it was time for the drought they had enough to last them until the rainy season. This new philosophy is giving back self-esteem and confidence to a nation, who had lost the will and know how, how to be entrepreneurial and as a result remained victims.

Like us, we all have potential to be and do anything we desire it is just having the L.U.C.K – location, understanding, contacts and knowledge.

Having it all

Many wealthy and rich people have a full and happy balanced life. There are also many rich people, who are not wealthy in the true sense. If they lost their cash, they would be left with few friends and be lonely sad soles.

I personally believe we can have it all. In my next book *'The Road to Wealth'* I expand on how this can be achieved and include true rags to riches stories. We are all ordinary people and ordinary people surround us, however we can all achieve extra-ordinary things, including achieving great wealth and financial freedom.

I would like you now to focus on your own wealth.
What do you have left in your life when you take away all the money?
- List your friends
- A favorite pet, car, outfit, shoes
- Your business contacts
- People of influence that respect you
- People that you know would help you out financially
- Banks or other businesses
- Your strengths
- Your skills that you have that are your trait
- Your experiences that make you unique, holidays, tragedies, good things, bad things
- The qualities that your friends think make you special
- Hobbies and skills
- Health and wellbeing
- Ideas and plans

When you start to make your list it quickly becomes bigger and longer and it is surprising how much is right in our lives. You need to keep this paper in your purse, diary or pinned up on your bathroom mirror, to remind yourself how special you truly are and how wealthy you are in all the areas of your life that truly count.

Its amazing that we **have so much** and yet only focus on what is missing!

This attitude of 'not enough' adds to dissatisfaction, whereas if we **focus on what is right.** – 'Voilá!' Like magic, we end up **being happier** and more satisfied each day. We can still desire more. It is human nature to have healthy goals to achieve. It is the fact that we now 'think differently' and as a consequence see the 'wealth' as wealth and feel more successful and more inspired to create more in and with our own lives.

Edward de Bono's comments

The gap between cope-space and demand-space (self-space and life-space) defines pressure or opportunity. It defines either the pressures that are exerted on an individual or the opportunity or challenge that is open to an individual. Since opportunity is positive and pressure is negative it is important to be able to distinguish between the two.
Deciding whether the gap is a pressure gap or an opportunity gap is a matter for individual thinking and perception and is one of the tasks expected of an individual in the Happiness Syndrome. Some guidelines can, however, be given:

Whether the gap is positive or negative may depend on the temperament of an individual – some enjoy challenge, some enjoy peace. The gap may change its appearance from positive to negative from day to day depending on the mood of the moment.

If the gap has been there for a *long time* and there has been no success in reducing it then it seems more sensible to regard it as a pressure than as an opportunity.

If a person considers himself or herself to be unhappy; then the gap is quite definitely a pressure. Happiness is defined as an approach towards a cope/demand ratio of unity – an exact fit between cope and demand.

chapter 7

Sexier Energy

TIP

A great relationship is like a great Tango dance…both peoples personalities flare up, both have a chance to take the lead, they have to trust, can be erotic and then gentle and comforting, daring, powerful, energising and loving…always with that tinge of excitement and unknowing…yet also knowing and trusting that the other will watch out for the others well-being. Just like good sex.

**SHELLEY SYKES
THE HAPPINESS GURU**

In my book '*Sexy Single & Ready to Mingle*' I make note that the more energy we have, the more attractive to others we become. High-energy people attract people to them like moths to a flame. Our smiles, our laughter, our zest for life is attractive and addictive. Our energy raises the mood of the room as we walk in.

People certainly want to spend more time with happy, high-energy people rather than those with a negative more morose outlook on life. We can all 'feel' the energies when we walk into a room if people have just had an argument. The saying is that 'you can cut the air with a knife' when the energies are negative.

Children's hospitals are colourful and upbeat places in comparison to that of the adult hospitals. Clowns are paid to bring laughter to the children's faces on the wards and the games that bring joy to children are also available.

Laughter is an excellent way to raise energies. In my survey for **Sexy Singles** and in my interviews of the **Lucky-in-Loves,** being able to laugh with one another was paramount and a major key to attraction.

Even in the corporate world, I hear more and more business entrepreneur's state that **they only do business with people that they like.** Most businesses only thrive despite having great products and services through great communication, building upon relationships with their suppliers and their customers as well as their own teams.

It is so important to keep our energies high for ourselves. For our health and for our own attractiveness. I call it sexy energy. To me energy attracts or detracts. Children, unless criticised a lot, always seem to have ample of this high energy. Life is full of possibilities for them. There are no limits as far as they can see. To them everything is a possibility, so they enjoy the moment full of joyful expectation. They don't question their actions saying:

- 'This is stupid' this isn't real
- This isn't going to happen
- I can't really fly or sing or dance
- What will my friends think?
- Will they laugh at me?
- This is a waste of time
- I'm not good enough
- I'm too young, too old, and too stupid…

Kids don't think what can go wrong, they **just create and do and enjoy** their creation and game playing and use their minds not to discourage themselves, but to **inspire new magic and thoughts of possibility.**

Catching **The Happiness Bug** keep people in the now and enjoy the present. It ensures pleasure for that moment, that day. Tomorrow is another adventurous day!

If we knew, whom we were going to meet and what was going to happen in our lives, it really could take out the sparkle and adventure of our lives, unless we create it.

I know many people who hate travelling, especially long distances by plane or train. I don't, because I always invariably meet new interesting people that I don't normally come into contact with. They sometimes become new friends, new business contacts or just interesting people that have given me a new perspective on life.

On a recent trip to Europe I flew via Kuala Lumpur to Amsterdam and was seated next to two Malaysian men. It was a night flight and so after many attempts to sleep 'comfortably' we were all awoken by the sound of the pilot and the chink of breakfast pots on the stewardess' trolley prior to landing. One of the men began small talk and just out of politeness I introduced myself and he responded that his name was Joy. "What a wonderful name" I said. He laughed and said a few of his European clients have a shock when he walks in – they expect a woman. We had another chuckle together. I found out that Joy worked for a Dutch company and travelled the world for them, particularly in Asia, his wife was expecting their second child and his birthday was 31st July. After a few more chuckles and introduction to the middle-man, Rav, Joy and I heard how Rav worked for a Belgium company specialising in sugary type solutions that were used in youth generation products, he had a loving wife and family although he had lost his mum to cancer and his birthday was on 30th July. Both men sympathised when I told them I was on my way to visit my mum in a Spanish hospital diagnosed with cancer... I was born on her birthday on July 29th! We all laughed when we realised we were sitting in line with consecutive July birthdays 29th, 30th, 31st respectively.

I took a photo of the three of us with my phone camera and we laughed even more. A connection was made that was unique to us. The flight and the last half an hour of the journey had been made more bearable with laughter amongst an unlikely three.

When they receive a birthday text and copy of the photo our bond will strengthen. I have no doubt that if I am in Malaysia I will be able to give them both a call and I will be greeted with a friendly and supportive warmth.

Whilst flying back from Spain to the UK I sat next to a young couple both 21 years old. Neither were doing jobs they liked. Both had been told by parents that they were better off getting 'good' jobs. He was a printer and bored and she worked in a solicitor's office. When I posed the question what would they do if it were possible to do something they loved... the young lady said write murder mystery books! Spooky I am author. It crossed my mind that I could be the catalyst that inspires this young lady to pursue her dream and just do it... plus she was dating a printer that could get her books printed. We all laughed at the synchronicity of it all and how possible everything was. He wanted to be an artist so being the 'Happiness Guru' I threw a few possibilities to them both, one being that he could ask if he could be transferred into the graphics department at work, whilst designing her book covers and that she use her solicitor's office for material to make her story lines accurate and have depth whilst writing her stories she would be being paid and building up material for her script.

The elation on their faces was worth all the time and effort to get to know a little about these 2 young people that could have settled for ordinariness all their lives. Now inspired with the knowing of possibilities I have no doubt that they will follow through and email me with their exciting news, happenings and successes.

Relationships are what dying people say they will miss – not the house or the cars, the clothes or the work... its their partner, the love of their cat or dog, their friendships and the fun and laughter of sharing experiences.

I had two days before I had to fly back to Sydney, after arriving in the UK from Spain. I was picked up by my two very special gay friends, Jonathon & Kevin at Midnight. It was wonderful to go back to their place and talk and find out about their dreams and aspirations – Kevin, the Opera Singing Star and Jonathon, the Teeth and Mouth surgeon. Both extremely talented, surprisingly though both doubting their abilities and worthiness… At 3 am we all retired with the possibility of dreaming about Kevin staring in The Phantom of the Opera, with Jonathon, me and his mum in front seats applauding him as well as seeing Jonathon being interviewed on TV about his work as a surgeon improving peoples self-esteem and confidence.

The next day they both giggled at breakfast, because they awoke that morning feeling happy and both felt elated at the possibility of being and doing what we had created the night before. They felt happier, they had a goal and a desire that was theirs and suited their skill set. It was now quite possible. Like most things it doesn't just 'fall' into your lap just because you 'dream about it', but life has a wonderful way of giving you what you need at the right time in the right way. It can even be better than you ever imagined!

Being open to the possibilities makes us more aware to new opportunities and we are more in tune to others that can be a link to our next part of our journey. It is quite exciting.

As humans we are programmed to create, as one dream and goal is achieved the next appears and we are forever moving forward and experiencing new dreams and possibilities.

For a long time I dreamt of living abroad in a place with blue skies and sunshine everyday. That dream and goal has been achieved and now my dreams and goals are focused on touching peoples lives through my books, TV and radio. I live in gratitude that I am living in a sunny land, where I want to be.

I am now open to the possibilities that relate to my dreams and goals and have no doubt that I will achieve them. The only thing I don't know is 'when' and my belief is that **'it will happen at the right time'**. So I am not 'worried' I just enjoy taking one step at a time, staying true to my dreams and goals. It is a massive relief not to have to 'worry' what if it does or doesn't or when it will happen – I trust that it just will!

Try it and see

Many worriers and sceptics may feel this is not possible. I say to you that it is. The best way to find out is to 'TRY IT & SEE' for yourselves. It only takes 21 days to get out of negative habits... By replacing negative attitudes and thought patterns with a new positive habitual attitude – life becomes a jollier place to be, even though to start with your experiences and present life conditions won't change immediately.

Friendships blossom, strangers start to talk to you and a calmness and confidence floods your persona. You no longer feel lonely with your own company. The benefits are amazingly wonderful.

The Prisoner and the Cat Story

In Sydney 1846 a man was thrown into a single dingy cell at the Rocks in Sydney for apparently stealing. He was left there to rot and was not fed. After many days of solitude the man, weak and lonely heard the throaty pure of a cat, who must have found it's way into the grate near the barred slit window of this man's cell. Instantly the man felt a wonderful sense of excitement. He started to make clicking noises to attract the cat. He spoke in a soft and encouraging voice. He didn't have a crumb to entice the cat, yet the cat gingerly allowed the man to stoke him. This lifted the man's spirits and having the company and ability to give love and compassion to another living thing was a worthwhile activity.

Each day the cat returned and after several days the cat started to bring tiny morsels of food to the prisoner! It was amazing that this cat kept this man alive!

Not only did the cat give this man sustenance, but also the cat gave this man a reason to live, friendship and ability to give love.

Eventually this man was allowed out of prison – even his captures were shocked and inspired by the generosity and camaraderie of this man and his stray cat.

Baby experiment in the 1950's Story

In the 1950's the scientists in the US wanted to see how touch and affection affected the well-being of infants from birth to one year olds. They took 50 orphaned babies and had nurses feed and hug and talk to these babies. They took another 50-orphaned babies and just fed and changed these babies, but these babies weren't hugged or spoken to.

Within weeks the second group of babies started to die on mass. It was such a shock, the experiment had to be stopped.

Nobody until this time had never realised how important hugs, love and affection was for our survival. Literally without it we curl up and die.

It has been proven that married or partners living together live far longer and have a happier life and existence than those living on their own. This news comes at a time when there are more than 50% of the population living alone.

As parents, it is our duty to love and comfort our children not just with words and gifts, but also with real physical hugs. Minimum hugs are 12 per day, but I reckon 60 hugs are better!

Filling your love bucket

After discovering these facts I make sure that I get my daily dose of hugs. When I am with friends and we do something great I insist on a group hug. At first some of my friends looked and probably felt awkward, but I would do it anyway. They would laugh and love it. It is a win-win, because they get hugged too. It feels great.
Now my friends just do it when I say and they still laugh and giggle. It's fun and feels good.

My teenage son despite being a teenager still likes to have his daily hugs. He even asks for one when he is feeling low. I call it **filling our love bucket!**
If you imagine we are like a big bucket with a tap near the bottom. Our bucket is filled with love juice and every time we do something for others we lose a little of our love juice from our tap. Every time we get criticised or condemned we also lose some of our love juice too from the tap. However every time we receive a hug, a compliment, do

something lovely for ourself, or feel good about ourselves for doing something lovely for others our bucket fills up a little more from the big tap of the universe.

Martyrs, which are many mothers of this world, are doing themselves a disservice, because they can only give as much as they have in their love bucket. A woman with a low self-esteem, who can't give herself self-love tends to give, but not get that much back. She survives on a sniff of a rag. If this mum has a few children they have to share this small amount of love juice and probably end up with a shortage of love and hugs that they deserve.

Many men who had parents that were critical and harsh tend to be the same on themselves and their families. It is hard to see people who are uncomfortable with touch and hugs, kissing and loving. **This can be changed though.**

People with **The Happiness Bug** tend to ensure that their love bucket is always filled by doing lovely stuff for themselves and those around them, maintaining high self-esteem and confidence. It is not only filled to the top, it begins to over flow so that they can help a lot more people by flooding their bucket. This is much better than just drip-feeding those around them.

Happy people tend to keep focused on filling their buckets to overflowing. They are buoyant and high-energy people with energy to spare to help more people.
These people, if they stop refilling their buckets will soon become low on energy and love to give others.

It is our purpose as 'Happy people' to keep our own **Love Buckets** filled.

TIP

Talking, listening, eye contact – feeling fascinated, happy and interested, more affectionate are all great signals to others that you care!

SHELLEY SYKES
THE HAPPINESS GURU

Edward de Bono's comments

Relationships

The paradox is that the great emphasis on self prevents selfishness, because other selves are regarded as equally important – that is the process of respect.

It must seem that a system that puts the highest emphasis on self as does the new Happiness Syndrome, would run into trouble with relationships. The traditional systems have tried to subjugate self, because self leads to selfishness and this upsets the relationship of man to his fellows and to society as well as to his salvation. The claim that self is all right up to a point and that then it becomes selfishness is impractical and weak and just a way of evading the issue.

The Happiness Bug system, which encourages selfishness, would suggest a laissez-faire system in which the strong triumph and the weak are subjugated. Paradoxically it is precisely, because the new Happy Bug system is so strongly in favour of self that the laissez-faire system is inappropriate.

The solution to the dilemma is quite straightforward. The emphasis on self applies not only to an individual's own self, but to all the different selves around him. **The emphasis on self-protecting his self, but also protects the others. The other selves include other people, but also the 'self' of the community and the social system.**

If for self we read 'system' then the new Happy System is in favour of the full functioning of a system without interference from other systems. The human systems are to function in parallel within the framework of the community and social system.

So by loving and living for the self it elevates the people around society, the community and us in a positive way.

chapter 8

Happy Success Stories

The real fact is that whatever your particular requirements are, there is probably someone out there that has those qualities. Just stay true to what you truly want.

**SHELLEY SYKES
THE HAPPINESS GURU**

Love, Luck, Looks and Laughter

If we ask most people what they want from life no matter where they live in the world they would generalise and answer in their own way: Love, Luck, Looks and Laughter.

Generally:

- Everyone wants to be loved and to love.
- Everyone wants to be prosperous if possible,
- Everyone wants good health and stay as attractive, young and as fit as possible for as long as it takes.
- Everyone wants to have fun and spend more time laughing.

It seemed till now that these four traits were only available to some lucky few, but with the fast contamination of **The Happiness Bug**, this is now spreading to all parts of the globe. Its properties are simple and quite virulent. It is a happy success story in it's own right.

From a world that was becoming a sick and a depressive society struggling with poverty and hunger. **The Happiness Bug** is inspiring people around the globe to contribute to:

- Relationship matching like dating agencies such as RSVP and Connect4Love and others are helping to fill the need to create a match for people to be able to live in love and share their life's journey and have someone special to laugh lots with.
- Create Worldwide Wealth such as leader Roger Hamilton of the XL Foundation and all its members as well as singer Bono, who wants to help put balance back into the world economies.
- 2B1 Charitable Foundation are about supporting every peoples, animals and the environment and The Worldwide Hunger Organisations are creating possibilities to teach and stop people suffering with hunger and starvation and people like Edward De Bono are setting the standard and leading the way to help people to think creatively and in harmony to work with others differences for a win-win scenario.
- Forever Young Clinics and many education establishments, TV, Magazines and Gurus including myself are supporting people to boost people's self-esteem and image, improving looks and health for a better quality of life.

The great thing is that none of us are alone. There is always someone that we can ask for help and advice (preferably someone that is where we want to be and has achieved what we aspire to achieve).

My biggest lesson was to 'allow others to help me'.
I had for many years been independent and proud. I wrongly thought that to ask for help meant I was weak and a failure. This is so not so.

TIP

Strong successful people **always ask for help** *so that they can grow faster and quicker.*

**SHELLEY SYKES
THE HAPPINESS GURU**

It had been a very expensive lesson for me, because for years I tried to do it all on my own and I realised I would have achieved so much more if only I had asked for help or support earlier.
The most successful people have had helping hands to get to where they needed to go. The great success story is that you and others will hopefully get the lesson without wasting any more time, if you're like me with this stubborn streak.

People feel great if they are needed and can help. It helps them fill their love bucket. You are doing them a favour by allowing them to support you!

Callum's Cure – Miracles do Happen Despite our Circumstances

14 years ago I was involved in a car crash in Holland, whilst pregnant. For 8 weeks I thought that this precious baby had died inside of me...because he no longer moved around as most foetuses do before gestation.

Fortunately for me he was born alive, albeit small and placed in an incubator for the first two weeks of his life. The shock of being a mum was tough, but the shock to being a mum of a sick baby was heart wrenching.

By week 6, according to all the books a baby was supposed to recognise its mother from the nipple – mine didn't. He recognised my voice, but had no reaction to purely visual stimuli. I took him to the doctors and insisted they make an appointment for him to be seen by a specialist.

After doing a CT scan it was confirmed that he had Cerebral Palsy – brain damage, which was affecting his eyes and would affect his mobility! I was gutted – yet made the decision to do what ever it would take to ensure that he would have the best chance medically and have a fun happy childhood.

I had his eyes operated on at 20 months and patched his eyes daily for 7 years.

He got the all clear on his vision at 8 years old! A happy outcome!

I did physiotherapy on his limbs every day and at 5 years old he took his first step unaided. At 6 years old he ran his first school race just like Forest Gump with callipers and at 8 years old I had his legs straightened so he could walk tall and be straight. The surgery was horrendous and the pain he want through phenomenal. It took a year to re learn to walk and at 9 he had straight legs! We moved to Sydney and for the very first time he was able to walk to his school!

Awesome happy outcomes! Anthony Robbins calls Callum Rory 'a miracle on legs!'

It isn't what happens to you in life that matters, its what you do about it that counts! Magic and Miracles do happen! 'Callum's Cure' is a best-selling book inspiring thousands.

Won a car!

Since moving to Australia Callum Rory has grown 3ft in height. At 14 years old he is 6ft tall and still growing. Because of these massive growing spurts Rory has had to have several operations on his legs to lengthen and help with his feet and ankle support. Each time his legs are in casts and he has to relearn to walk. Earlier this year he had to have his 4th operation and I just knew that there was no ways that I would be able to fit him, with his long legs in casts into my two-seater sports car plus the wheel chair. I would definitely need a 4-wheel drive. My sports car was a special import we brought with us to Australia and it had a restriction on selling it . . . it would take months to get the all clear from Canberra to release the restrictions I was told.

One day as I was contemplating who I knew who had a 4-wheel drive that we may be able to borrow, I walked in to the local post office and the lady behind the counter greeted me with great enthusiasm. "Shelley, you have won a car!" My heart leapt, but when we checked the parcel Nestlé was doing a promotion. I had won a box of their Cheerio's cereals and the potential to win a 4-wheel drive Honda Rav. Being the Happiness Guru and the eternal optimist, I took this as an excellent sign and enrolled all my friends to eat Nestlé chocolate bars for a week so that we could submit the wrappers in time for the competition deadline.

I was so certain we were going to win, because every day we kept seeing this particular 4-wheel drive in the promotion. They travelled in front of us, behind us; parked at the side of us ... Rory and I were amazed!

I was so sure that we were going to win, that the day of the Nestlé draw I stayed at home ready to take the call. It never came. I decided to work from home the next day just in case they had to call after processing all the entries. The call never came. On Wednesday I must admit I was feeling let down, disappointed and concerned I had not resolved our transport problem.

On the Thursday I went to work as normal – I worked late that day and when I returned home I had several messages, none from Nestlé. One however was from Hallmark Cards. I thought perhaps they wanted to ask for permission to use some of my quotes for their cards or if not, ask me to speak. I rang the next day and the lady asked if I was sitting down. I was curious and replied I was. She then announced, "You are the family winner of our Fathers Day Promotion and have won a Ford Escape 4-wheel drive."
You can imagine, I whooped with joy and babbled on how marvellous this would be for my son's wheel chair after the operation. I couldn't remember what the Escape looked like ... she said 'big and black'.

She said she would phone me back later. As soon as she hung up I phoned my best friends who had helped munch Nestlé bars. Chris ran out of work and screamed down the telephone in excitement. Her husband phoned a few minutes later confirming he thought I was mad, when I had first told him I was going to win the 4 wheel drive – he was delighted I had. Lisa and her partners were equally thrilled for Rory and I and said it couldn't have happened to two better people for a great and worthwhile cause. I felt so grateful.

When the lady called back she went on to say there were some formalities to complete before the handover of the vehicle... receipt of the card from Coles supermarket.

My heart sank! It all came back to me. I had bought my dad a father's day card a week before fathers day and noticed Coles and Hallmark were doing a competition. This one had been simple. Buy a card and SMS name and number as well as the bar code of the card for the opportunity to win! I had SMS'ed that same night before posting the card to England.

I never kept my Coles receipts and normally I paid cash. The administrator at Hallmark insisted that the receipt was imperative and made the competition legal.

We were so close – there had to be a way.

I phoned Coles and made an appointment to see the manager. My dad re-posted the card back to Australia as proof of purchase and for the barcode too. Once the Coles manager had had a call from the Hallmark company administrator confirming that I had been picked a winner subject to the receipt, it took several days before verifying my wonderful win... together we worked back to the date I thought I had bought the card. We found it, June 8th at 7.39pm. I had paid on my visa card! The joy and relief were fantastic, because Coles were able to supply me with a duplicate receipt.

It took several more weeks before the car was available for pick up. The Ford Escape looked brilliantly shiny outside the show room ready for me to drive off.

The first stop was the post office! I parked the car outside and joined the long queues. I hoped I would be served by the lady, who had first inspired me to enter the competitions, unfortunately I ended up at the end counter, so I whispered to the man serving, to tell Linda at the end, that I had won the car! All the counter staff passed on the message and lost all concentration. The queues behind me were long and becoming restless. They knew something was going on, but when she screamed at the news I just jumped around facing the whole mass of people and burst out with my amazing news and announced I was a winner of a 4-wheel drive car! Everyone were surprised and stunned, but in true Aussie fashion cheered and clapped. The post office was a hub of energy and possibility. Everyone went out to look at the car! People love happy stories.

The wheel chair was a perfect fit! It was a 'God-send' for Rory and I, to get about after his leg operation.

Another very Happy Story! Magic and miracles do happen!

24 year old wins European Lottery

Now I am not saying everyone should enter all the competitions to win things – but if you don't enter you don't win.

I have always entered the National Lottery, because my very small donation helps some lucky person to become a millionaire and also a large percentage of the money is given to the charities, which really benefit. I obviously hope to win the jackpot myself and I am thrilled to hear of winners, but I don't rely on the outcome just like Daniel.

Daniel and his girlfriend finally made the decision to move to Australia to live and work. Daniel's girl friend is a nurse and she found work in the first week at the city hospital. It had been a big decision for Daniel to move countries, because he wasn't the natural adventurous type, but when his family received a call from Daniel announcing he was flying back home to the UK they were a bit shocked he hadn't given Australia more of a go. It had only been two weeks, since they left the UK! Then it suddenly dawned on them that something terrible must have happened!

"No we're both fine" said the 24 year old "its just that I am the jackpot winner of the European Lottery fund and need to fly back to settle the paper work!!"

You can imagine the stunned silence on the end of the phone!

24 years old and now a millionaire! How fabulous. They are set for life if they invest wisely. Now, back in Australia they are living a wonderful life – their dream life. It's just perfect for them!

Too many people make judgements what you should and shouldn't do. I think there are no right or wrong ways. Do what is right for you and your family. Daniel may invest in a business that succeeds and employ lots of workers to help them achieve their dreams. His increased wealth will mean he can give more to charities and the community. What comes around goes around.

Some one always wins! Why not you? Good luck!

The Note Book – True Love

I watched this movie on a plane to Amsterdam – crying, laughing and sighing at the romantic loving parts. This is about true love to the max! I knew at the end I wanted a man like the lead to want to love me as much as this man loved his wife. It is about their love story, their true passion keeping strong, through sickness and health, through troubled times and despite the obstacles.

The ending was a happy one, because they were truly together in peace, but at the same time sad. I could not stop crying for half an hour after the movie had finished, it touched me so much. I didn't care that the other passengers were looking at me, I felt inspired that such love could be captured so well on film – a truly happy, honest love. I recommend everyone watch it, especially lonely singles or those in relationships accepting unacceptable treatment. Watching this movie will definitely inspire you to raise your standards and be expectant for the right person to come into your life.

Olympic Champions – Despite Personal Injury

Most people enjoy watching the Olympic Games, where world champion athletes compete against one another to beat one another for the prize of a Gold medal and world recognition, ultimately beating existing world records. It is a series of games of intenseness, because the entrants are so focused, so highly tuned from hours, days, weeks, months and years of practice. These people are dedicated. Their strength comes from their mind and their bodies. If either go wrong – wow it can be mentally devastating and physically gruelling, because of the adrenaline addiction to the exercise and the thrill they get from actually taking part in doing what they love. These players are certainly passionate about their sport.

I interviewed Kerrie-Anne Pothharst one of Australia's Beach Volley Ball Olympians, who earlier on in her career tore a leg muscle and injured her knee cartilage, whilst playing basketball. She looked doomed to never play competitive sport again. She was devastated. But her boyfriend at the time bought her a beach volleyball and wrote on each strip of leather a goal, walk, swim, reach touch, bend, cycle, run . . . Everyday she looked at her ball, touched her goals, whilst she was laid up and visualised herself walking until she was strong enough to stand. Every day she took action to achieve the first goal and when that was done aimed for the next. With beautiful long firm legs this lady achieved the impossible and not only became strong, she became a powerhouse, someone to be reckoned with on the beach during the Olympics using visualisation to see that gold medal around her neck!

 **TIP**

Even under extreme competition and against all the odds,
if the will and the desire are there to take action,
anything is possible.

SHELLEY SYKES
THE HAPPINESS GURU

Anthony Robbins – Rags to Riches

Many of you reading this book may have already heard of Anthony Robbins and some may have been to one of his seminars or heard his CD's. He is a 6ft 7 good looking giant, who became a millionaire by 19 years old. He had very humble beginnings coming from a tough working class family. When the going got really tough his dad left home and so this young Tony was left helpless, but determined never to be so poor again. He did what ever it would take to learn from the masters, who were creating wealth, even taking a job as a janitor and living in his car, whilst studying professional speakers, who where making a difference to peoples lives and getting paid handsomely for it.

Life hasn't been smooth sailing, since making his first million. As we all know sometimes we have to lose that, which is most precious to us to appreciate how lucky we were and are. Anthony however is persistent and driven to help others achieve their potential dreams, goals, health and lifestyle.

Over the years he has mastered his techniques and those of others that he knew would make a difference to his audiences, whether they be the President of the United States, the military, world tennis champions or ordinary people wanting to achieve extra ordinary things. Anthony has now attracted great fortunes for himself and his family, a healthy lifestyle, owns a sanctuary in Fiji, a foundation for teenagers and travels the world speaking and touching peoples lives in an entertaining, high energy way – my kind of man! He is living his dream life and walking his talk. He has unleased his power from within and is now sharing how with others. www.anthonyrobbins.com

Dolphin Man's Story – Death and Dreams

Andrew found his soul mate Pippa, married her and they built their dream house together. She was the high-powered business lady and he was the lovable creative carpenter. They were one another's Ying and Yang, a balanced relationship – when she was stressed he would be calm; when he got frustrated she would be his peace and tranquil love. They had their first love child Matt, followed shortly by twins, Finn and Luke – three boys before she was diagnosed with cancer. She lasted three years before passing on. Leaving a grieving husband and 3 beautiful baby boys. Andrew was gutted.

18 months later he is the adoring dad that everyone wants – Organised, demonstrative, loving and caring. Roguishly good looking, a gem for any girly to want to nurture and care for, but this man is energised. He has a dream and a passion to swim with Dolphins every day if he can and take people into the wonderful world of the Dolphins and Whales in order to help heal them and yet feel and enjoy the magic.

My son and I had the privilege of swimming with the Dolphins with Andrew, his boys and his team off the coast of Nelson Bay Port Stephens just 2.5 hours drive north of Sydney. It was the most beautiful thrilling experience.

Andrew has a dream and 2B1 Charitable Foundation is supporting that goal, to take trips out weekly to help educate people into self love and belief, healthier living and caring and learning from these most magnificent creatures.

His wife's death has awakened in him the gift of treasuring every moment and to pursue what he loves doing the most. Swimming with the Dolphins and sharing this gift with others and enjoying his boys. Check out his website www.dolphcom.com.au

Dr John Demartini – Break Through

John was a typical schoolboy that had a few learning difficulties, now labelled dyslexia. The more the teachers chastised him, the more anxious he became. When these god-like adults told him he was stupid and hopeless he unfortunately began to believe them and like most kids his age, his self-esteem plummeted when he took their words seriously. The only thing he knew he was good at was surfing. At thirteen years old his dislike of being chastised and restrictions of the school system had reached its peak and he told his parents he was leaving home to find his fortune as a surfer. They surprisingly (or perhaps not, living with a 13 year old teenager isn't that easy) drove him to the highway so that he could begin his hitchhike up the coast.

No boy should be living on the streets and doing it tough. John did and survived. Somehow he met a fellow, who inspired him to learn to read and to study the mind and body. He told John that anything was possible. John took this kind man's words to heart.

John today has read more books than anyone alive probably, speaks to 300 audiences a year and touches peoples lives and inspires them to break through their limiting belief patterns. A very successful, affluent businessman, a qualified chiropractor (he no longer practices), instead he is now known as a philosopher and speaker.

John's own experiences once again shows that we can achieve if we believe! The past does not equal the future.

Branson's Brainstorm

It is a fact that most millionaires don't have a degree qualification. They have made their financial wealth with an idea they followed through on and persisted with despite setbacks. The one common denominator is that they all had or have an idea that they were or are passionate about creating into reality.

Richard Branson was told by teachers 'he was not clever' and could end up in prison. Now one of the wealthiest most respected and ethical business entrepreneurs of our time, with businesses in music, finance, cosmetics, travel, communications and hopefully Anti-Aging Clinics and TV shows . . . (I have plans he doesn't know about yet! Ha Ha!) This man affects change. He embraces a challenge and loves creating possibilities for the betterment of mankind and our planet in a fun way. He may not have been academically 'clever,' but he is certainly SMART. Most millionaires are. They know which 'clever' people to ask to help them achieve their goal. Smart people don't need to have to know everything, they don't need to know how things will work, and they just need to know how to 'ask for help'.

One of Richard's great skills is attracting ordinary people to his team and allowing them to flourish in a 'loving, creative environment' so that they become amazing people. He attests his success is mainly due to the great people in his teams. He honours them for themselves, with or without certificates to their name. He allows people to develop their ideas and helps many people around the world realise their own dreams.

I recently had the pleasure of hearing Richard address a group of small business owners in Sydney. What really amazed me was this mans humbleness, despite his great achievements, completing on his goals and financially achieving great wealth despite the risks and fear that dream making often entails. His appetite for change and possibility was inspirational. His creativity undiminished. When I had the audacity to ask him for funding for a global TV show, he laughed and was open to possibilities... you can imagine my excitement!

What touched my heart though, was Richard's desire to contribute and utilise his influence and power to help world leaders empower one another and embrace a position of responsibility that doesn't entail politics for the betterment of everyone's daily living around the world. His mission is to help reduce conflict.

In his own words "people like Nelson Mandela will not be around forever, but their wisdom and respect defies politics and nations and borders, religions and cultures". The hairs down the back of my neck pricked up, because my beloved friend Edward de Bono the inventor of lateral thinking and conflict resolution expert has a similar dream and has already built a World Thinking Centre for world leaders on an island off the shores of Malta. Had these two men met? No.
Edward would make a perfect elder on this committee. My goal was then to introduce these two amazing visionaries to effect world peace and possibilities!

As synchronicity has it, both are flying into Sydney in August/ September. Edward is coming to this 'Happiness Bug' Book launch! The dream plan is for the three of us arriving to the launch party at the Botanic Gardens by air balloon with bubbles and butterflies being released out in to the guests below . . . Walt Disney would love the plan. However, due to aviation laws, it will probably most likely be somewhere happy and serene like the Chinese Gardens.

Success is so much sweeter when you are having fun, whilst on the journey of converting your dreams into reality!

Michael Jackson's Music

At home I have a pictorial mosaic of how my life is and will be. Michael Jackson's picture is on there and it always provokes questions of why, by guests that see it, especially at this time when Michael has gone through the grinder over unsubstantiated allegations that have had a very damning effect on his life and career. Many people are so quick to judge and drop creative people like hotcakes when the going gets tough. Not me. I have no idea whether Michael did or didn't do the things that he is accused of. My belief is, that he is a most talented man, yet a misunderstood man. It is my opinion that he has a heart of gold where children are concerned and I choose to believe that he has been misjudged. Like Sir Isaac Newton, geniuses are often critisised as heretics because of their non-conformity to social expectations.

Like Michael, I just love music, it changes my state and it certainly is a big part of my life. I listen to it and dance to it every day. Michael has a wonderful gift that he has deliberately honed to produce up beat, funky easy to dance to music. Even his videos are masterpieces of creativity. I have followed his career with admiration, love and respect. When I play his music I can't help but jiggle my feet and my hips. It makes me want to buggy-on-down, even if a minute before I was feeling despondent, lethargic or down about something.

I just love dancing...it takes my mind off situations and I become conscious of being in the present.

I was fortunate to win a Disco Dance championship in South Africa when I was younger and it started me on the career of TV and the media. The 'rhythm' is in me. I am passionate about dance and music. I think music is one of the best mediums to teach people about joy and life. It is one of the ways I communicate. We have all seen blacks despite their environments smile and laugh when they are singing and dancing. They know the secret to being present and how to enjoy music for its uplifting and happy state it brings. Just like kids and our teenagers. Perhaps grown-ups need to listen to more music!

I still have a dream to dance with Michael Jackson on stage one day and not surprisingly, I believe it will happen. I have an expectation it will. I don't know how, when or where, but I know it will.

Michael's life has certainly not been all sunshine. His good and bad experiences have certainly made him the person he is today. His highs have been humungous and yet his lows nobody would wish on their enemy. The result is a sensitive caring compassionate person, a great dad, a great musician/singer a creator, a humble human with unusual and unique ways.

Like Bart Simpson says "Damned if you do and damned if you don't." Michael will, I am sure continue to weave magic with his music and continue to rise like a phoenix out of the flames of societies wrath to heavenly heights and I will be dancing all the way!

Eminem's Eurhythmics

Eminem was my inspiration to write and perform a Rap Song to a group of 800 – 14 to 18 year olds in San Diego...

Mama I never want to hurt you
I never want to make you cry...

I was to speak on positive parenting to these young adults, who probably had never received positive parenting in their lives. They were lucky if they had even been parented, many coming from homes or juvenile centres. My message was that 'The past doesn't equal the future, magic and miracles do happen despite our circumstances'.

I became 'the oldest rapper' according to my grandma aged 98 (still helping 'old people' younger than herself at the centre), who on hearing I was the 'Rapping Mama' declared me 'too old to be one'.

On reflection, I realised I had been very brave changing my whole speech the night before my presentation at an Anthony Robbins camp, to perform to this mass of underprivileged, aggressive, adolescent group of youths by donning a big hooded sweat shirt from a teen in the audience, large basketball pants and someone's size 23 trainers 'to look like them' and their hero Eminem!

My son who was 10 years old at the time, warmed up the crowd by announcing 'he had started life blind and had been ear marked to never be able to walk according to doctors. He was classified 'disabled', but he had defied the odds with the thanks to his mum.' It was strange the change in the audience. Rory considered himself better off to be disabled and to have gone through surgery after surgery, than to have been sexually or physically abused. The audience looked on and suddenly realised that 'they were lucky' that they had only suffered sexual and physical abuse and not been born 'disabled'!

The transition from being a victim to being lucky and grateful was powerful.

They all related to being labelled 'bad' or 'a no hoper'. So they energetically began to follow my son Rory's prompts when he asked them to 'beat box' as I entered onto the stage.

The room was electric when I strutted on and began to wrap to the beat of their beat-boxing sounds.

I know that most of you think that Eminem is king,
Cos he made it big & he can sorta sing,
I've done it tough,
I've made it good, but none of us are the same,
I'm the Rappin Mama

The oldies in the room don't understand Rap,
So this is our underground tune,
Parent potential still exists, but to tell you the truth
it's oh so rare,
Most are immune,
I'm the Rappin Mama

My Gingerbread boy has brought me so much joy,
So I made a pact; as a matter of fact,
To be the best mommy for my son Callum Rory

Chorus...

Life is never always fair,
Take control and be aware

When you're feeling down and you're alone
Look inside you and it's there
Ha ha ha ha I'm the Rappin Mama

I'm not a great cook so I wrote a book,
On positive parenting,
My recipes for happy kids, goes like this:
(I change into Mary Poppins at this point …)
Huge amounts of self-esteem with oodles of confidence
Buckets of love and great self-belief,
Makes for happy kids and societies relief.

Chorus …

Life is never always fair,
Take control and be aware
When you're feeling down and you're alone
Look inside you and it's there
Ha ha ha ha I'm the Rappin Mama

Most young dudes are quick and bright,
They love their oldies with all their might,
Sometimes it hurts, it's not that easy,
Without great leaders to build us up,
I'm the Rappin Mama

Listen to me and be your best
Use your intuition you know the rest,
Trust your gut and you'll go far,
Dream big dreams,
Expect the bizarre!
I'm the Rappin Mama

All went well until I stripped off on stage to the horror of some of the Anthony Robbins organisers. They realised soon enough I was wearing my own 'Modern-day Mary Poppins' outfit as I continued in a Julie Andrews sing song voice...

I managed to get through my wrap perhaps not as smoothly as I would have liked – it was the first performance, but the message was loud and clear to the teenagers that I was truly attempting to connect with them in their language.

Everyone in the audience roared with applause. Rory and I were shocked at the mass support.

I waited for the silence before I went on with the rest of my presentation about the **desire and will to make a difference** to Rory's life and my own. You could have heard a pin drop.

I explained that the struggle that we all go through on life's journey actually makes us unique and special and **that anything is possible** even getting the blind to see and the disabled to walk if the determination and drive and desire is strong enough. We can all create our own magic in our lives despite our circumstances...just like Eminem. **They could achieve anything they desired despite having a bad start in life, or parents that didn't care. That was the past, no body can take away your dreams unless you let them and magic does happen.**

Well from that day forward Rory was called 'Rocking Rory' and I was Rappin Mama'. The audience slapped us, clapped us and gave us hugs during the rest of our stay at the camp. They expressed their desire that they wanted the book *Callum's Cure'* to be published and urged that I produce the rap single! It was suggested that the single be included in the back of each book, so parents got the book and the kids got the message from the music.

Their wish then became my reality!

The book was first published by Simon & Schuster and Anthony Robbins added his testimonial – a must read.

The book is currently being converted into a movie script in the US!

Not only did I produce the single with the talented help of my friend Nick, we produced a DVD with the help of Rory's friends, my clients and the talented skills of editors from Fox Studios.

Eminem has a lot to answer for!

He himself is a passionate man, victimised and yet created, because of his challenging journey – an orator to the youth. His power, I think on many occasions has even shocked him to the core. Despite his stardom he has his challenges and he shares his issues through his music, just like Edward and I with our books, speaking engagements, TV and 'our' happy music!

It won't surprise you then, when I say I will be rapping with Eminem, this great Rapping oracle . . . as Rappin Mama when I get to the USA. He has a lot more to give and he now, more than any other time realises, he too can make a positive difference to the lives of the many listeners of his music.

Instead of 'grown-ups' trying to suppress such artists we should be embracing them to help inspire the kids to become their best and to learn from our mistakes so they can get to where they need to be quicker and easier. Apple Music Company certainly knows the advantage of such an alliance. It is a proven fact that kids learn best through music and are influenced by people that they admire and respect. Sometimes we have to take the rough with the smooth. Truly, I dislike swearing. I 'get it' however, that this form of expression is easily translated as anger and frustration. It is a side that I personally don't choose to pursue; yet many teenagers get empowered and feel heard when they themselves don't yet have the communication skill, vocabulary or maturity to express their emotions eloquently. The simplistic vocals of a swear word suffice.
There is no right or wrong. It just is.

We are all connected. Our job is to know how best to communicate with one another effectively so that our messages are heard and understood. Thanks to Eminem and his incredible connection with the teenagers and young adults, I was able to emulate him and get my message across – in a Rappin' Mama sorta way!

 **TIP**

Remember there are no rules that are right or wrong. There are more ways to do what we need to do, we just have to find the one that is appropriate for whom we are communicating with.

SHELLEY SYKES
THE RAPPIN HAPPINESS GURU

Many grown-ups listening to my Rappin Mama song and still don't get it, but the kids and teenagers do and that's what counts.

Trust your gut and you'll go far,
Dream big dreams,
Expect the bizarre...

And perhaps you will be able to sing with your favourite pop idol. Anything is possible!

Don Tollman's Memory Skills

Don is described as the 'Indiana Jones of health'. He wears his cowboy hat and black handlebar moustache with pride. He is a kind and fun-loving guy that tells his story as it is, almost disguising his brilliance. He starts his presentations with a mind game getting someone from the audience to write 26 words that he glimpses, for literally 5 seconds and then is able to resight – front wards, backwards and in any order. We are transfixed – how does he do that?

His story is equally amazing. As a little boy he was described of average intelligence. He just liked playing – a wild child. One day he decided to try out a Sunday school class – just to see what went on. It was story telling from the bible. On that day he was told the story of Daniel and how the king wanted special kids to live and learn under his care to become the future leaders. Some of the children refused to eat the king's delicious foods. They wanted to eat just fruits and vegetables with a special meal of pulse. These children at the end of one year seemed to be stronger, healthier and brighter than all the other students – so the king announced that all students would be put on the same type of eating plan.

Don was impressed and wanted to be stronger and a smarter boy too, but no one seemed to know what this special meal was, not the teacher, nor the vicar or any other specialists. It became a life long obsession to find out.

Don's quest has had him searching in the pyramids of Egypt, learning how to read sacred scripts and studying cultures far and wide.

As luck would have it, after a chance meeting at an airport many many years later Don met with a man, who was needing someone to employ – a person to help categorise many ancient artefacts that his family had collected as investments over many years. Don jumped at the chance to take up the job and so it was during one of these days of checking through the boxes he came across a translated script that described this ancient meal of pulses and fruits and their association to the body, mind and soul. The elusive recipe had finally fallen into his lap!

Don has become an expert in health and wellness in his humorous and fun loving way and works with the top scientists of the world that are now validating the energy and vital benefits that these food substances have on our mind, body and soul. He explains how the ancients knew and practiced ways of learning without the rostrum of linea learning and how through eating and drinking special fruits and vegetables it empowers the body and keeps it fit and healthy. He describes how certain foods have signatures to represent different parts of our bodies for example:

Avocados: Take 9 months from seed to fruit and are great for women with uterus or fertility problems.

Walnuts: Are great for the brain and even look like them

Carrots: For the eyes and its signature have the look of the eye.

His dream is to inspire people to look after their minds and bodies so that they live fuller healthier happier lives. Its exciting stuff and I have no doubt he will make a massive impact. His compendium of health, that he describes as a family heirloom, which can be purchased off my website www.shelleysykes.com and is a comprehensive guide to the teachings of the ancients about herbs and formula for healing and being healthy.

For more information check out his website www.dontolman.com

Edward de Bono's comments

Humour

It has always surprised me how little attention philosophers have paid to humour, since it is a more important process of mind that is reason.

In this respect humour is regarded in two different ways that are distinct and yet come together in the end. The first way is as an attitude to life. The second way is as a key process in perception. We can now look in a general way at the reasons behind the elevation of humour to a position usually reserved for more solemn matters.

Humour is positive and life enhancing. The purpose of humour is enjoyment and happiness. Humour is anti-solemnity. In place of fervour and intensity the new Happy system would place the liveliness of humour and its relaxation.

Humour is anti-arrogance. Humour is for tolerance and humility. You listen to someone else's story and he will listen to yours. Arrogance is a fundamental 'sin' in the new Happy system. Humour offers a proto-truth for a very brief instant. We accept humour for what it is.

Humour is accessible. You do not have to be a genius or a saint to have a sense of humour.

Humour arises directly from that process of perception, which allows the mind to switch over and look at something in a completely new way.

Negative aspect of humour

There is a minor negative aspect of humour that perhaps ought to be considered. Because it is possible to laugh or sneer at everything it might seem that nothing is ever worth and the only solution is to drift along without effort or activity. This attitude to humour is similar to the negative and critical attitude of mind that has been discussed in earlier sections. The sneer is false humour. The true attitude is the deliberate putting on of fancy dress and enjoying it, knowing that it may be ridiculous if you choose to regard it as such, but not minding.

chapter 9

Pros, Cons & Contributions

> *Whatever you believe comes true and you are right,*
> *positive or negative.*
>
> **SHELLEY SYKES**
> **THE HAPPINESS GURU**

What are the 'prospects' for being contaminated with The Happiness Bug?

Life is certainly a series of pressures and opportunities. It depends on individuals what they perceive as a pressure or a pleasure. Edward has already described the perceived differences of pressure or opportunity. Our perception then is key to our happiness and with **The Happiness Bug** many of our pressures turn into opportunities or pleasures. For example I love presenting and speaking and yet for some people this would be their biggest nightmare. They are filled with fear at the thought, they would prefer death than to stand up in front of a group of people and speak.

If a person believes that speaking is a scary thing to do and they imagine themselves failing and being laughed at – it becomes their reality and truth. It would be scary to get up there and speak. I on the other hand look forward to speaking, because I visualise that my message will be understood, appreciated and inspirational. I visualise success and joy, a win-win scenario for us all and I speak from the heart and trust that I am heard through hearts.

What research has shown and I have noticed, however is that people who can visualise positive outcomes normally succeed better, than those that 'hope' for positive outcomes. And definitely better than those who expect things to happen, but don't do anything about it. People who have been contaminated with the 'Happiness bug' are more trusting in life's patterns – they visualise a happier out-come. People with a definite purpose tend to feel the fear and so do it anyway. Many of what appeared to be pressures, become reduced and neutralise or swing in favour of being an opportunity or pleasure.

What are the consequences for being contaminated?

The resultant consequences are:

- Reduction in stress
- Increased visualisation skills
- Energy levels increase
- Less likely-hood of procrastination
- Feeling of gratitude and appreciation

- Calmness that all is well
- Wonderment at what the lesson is next
- A feeling of connectedness
- Attraction to other amazing high-energy happy people
- Continual feeling of wellness
- A happier state.

When the 'contaminated' of **The Happiness Bug** are about, you automatically want to be with them. It is more fun, energising and things 'get done.'

When we attract others into our realm, lives and ideas intermingle. We create opportunities together that on our own would never have formulated so it is very exciting.
I certainly believe there is a book to be written by every one of us. Our stories and perceptions on life are unique. Before writing my first book, I read avidly and admired and respected those authors for touching me in some way. Their skill seemed so 'special' and I assumed it would be 'hard work' to write a book. I thought it would take months perhaps years, not weeks!

The secret is that nothing is hard work if you are passionate about it. No matter what your PASSION is for YOU, it will not seem hard. Life will flow, time will pass you by, people will come into your life synchronistically based on your focus and wealth and prosperity will magically appear.

In 2006 Harvard Business School announced that in the first half of the year, 87% of all new businesses were being set-up by women. Many women leaving the corporate world, where rigidity and male dominance in top ranking positions still reigns – these ladies are looking out for an opportunity to follow their passion and enjoy a 'work-style' that fits around their 'home-style.' Other types of women perhaps being those, needing to be mums yet yearning to keep their finances or individuality on track are starting home businesses too. They used to be called cottage businesses, but now a days some of these home run businesses are so profitable and attracting massive revenues they are putting the big companies to shame – often companies that over looked these savvy ladies, whilst they were in their employ. Pressure for these ladies has definitely been changed into opportunity and for the majority, pleasure, running businesses that are really their passion.

It is the same if you are writing your book on your life experiences, your message of enlightenment, your favourite topic, hobby or interest.

Since writing my first book my focus has obviously turned to authoring. Well bless my cotton socks! I seem to have attracted a whole bevy of authors as my friends – each author **passionate** about their message. Each one, **focused** on '**making a difference**' and yet each one of us seems to be saying similar messages about:

Life Beyond Limits – Infinity belief	Rik Schnabel
Your attitude Determines Your Altitude	Fabrizio Poli
Screw it, let's do it	Richard Branson
Unleash the Power Within	Anthony Robbins
Wink and Grow Rich	Roger Hamilton

The Psychology of Success	Brian Tracy
Energy, Enthusiasm, Excellence	Sajeela Cormack
Time to Kick But!	Rosemary Pekar
The 6 Dimensions of top Achievers	Dave Rogers & Arthur Carmazzi
Six Thinking Hats	Edward de Bono
Better than Chocolate	Siimon Reynolds
The Break through Experience	Dr John Demartini
You don't have to be born brilliant	John McGrath
Follow your Heart	Andrew Mathews
Hope Happens	Catherine Devrye
Walking Tall	Lesley Everett
The 12 Disciplines for Living Your Dreams	Bob Urichuck
Selling You	John C Jacob

...being a member of the National Speakers Association... I have a whole list of amazing speaker/author friends – too many to list here, but all equally effective and passionate (we are like a tribe...)

Each one of us experienced something that urged us to create our story and let our message inspire, teach, educate and enlighten. Perhaps, you are now inspired to start writing your own book!

What can we as the 'contaminated' contribute to society by being infected?

We can all Make A Difference and as a team the effect is often greater and more widespread. This empowers us to do more for others. The more we achieve to 'make a difference', the more we want to do.

Edward De Bono and I wanted to 'make a difference' on a global scale and so we started the 2B1 Charitable Foundation. It's a charity organisation that has the flexibility to support an array of causes around the planet including other organisations, as well as the individual, who often is left out once the charities become big and political.

One People, One Nation, One Earth, One Planet – **2B1**

A worldwide organisation based in Sydney, Australia – Set up to **make a difference** to those in need:

- Individuals
- Communities
- Other Charitable Organisations
- The Environment
- Planet Earth
- The Animals and Sea Creatures

...we are all one.

One People, One Nation, One Earth, One Planet – **2B1**

I had a dream and a goal to set up a flexible and free charity. **2B1** was founded in 2006 with Edward de Bono. I started active contribution after I had been involved in a serious car accident, whilst pregnant. As you now know, my son Callum Rory was born blind and the doctors said he would never see or walk.

I was determined to do everything I could to help him achieve the impossible with the help of dedicated individuals at the hospital. I began to fund raise for the hospital so they could continue helping other families, each year by holding a Beautiful Charity Ball sponsored by local businesses and my expansive network of friends. Rory now sees and walks – **Anthony Robbins** calls him a miracle on legs.

After moving to Sydney, I was asked to help out with 6 children's charities by hosting big charity ball events. Due to the politics and the restrictions these organisations had I found that individuals were not receiving the support, only the organisations as a group and the charities were very limiting and restrictive by the charities own constitutions.

2B1 gives companies and individuals the opportunity to select, which charities their money is directed too, if they deposit on a regular basis and it also gives significance to people, that their money is 'Making A Difference' in real need cases from projects with the planet arc, to swimming with Dolphins or helping individuals in need.

Edward and I decided that we would contribute 10% of all our book sales to the **2B1 charity**. My son and I even contribute 10% of our earnings and so do all the companies I am associated with. We are part of the XL Worldwide Wealth campaign for community care and feel wealthier for it. We love being MAD and want to be MADDER . . . making a bigger difference!

How you can Make A Difference? M.A.D.

You can help by donating some of your time, fundraising or donating part of your income, even purchasing products. Just a kind gesture or smile to someone makes a difference.

2B1 would love you to be one of our fund raising teams or set up your own direct debit to 2B1 foundation and donate 10% of your earnings or company turnover to provide funds for your favorite groups and help make a difference to individuals and causes for a better life on this, our wonderful earth.

We are all connected – 2B1

When we help others we help ourselves

Richard Branson has a Virgin Foundation and donates large proportions of his massive wealth to charities.

Anthony Robbins formed the Anthony Robbins Foundation and Basket Brigade to help youth and the families in need.

Bill Gates gives away $100's of millions to charities every year.

Roger Hamilton started the Worldwide Wealth Campaign.

Bono has his charity campaign to rebalance the wealth distribution too.

Oprah gives away $10's of millions to charities every year too.

TIP

*When I lost all my money I realised that when I gave
I no longer felt poor!
When you get used to giving when you have less,
it is easier to give when rich.
When you have more wealth you can give a lot more!
When you give a lot more,
you get a lot more in so many ways.*

SHELLEY SYKES
THE HAPPINESS GURU

My mission is to attract and create billions of dollars, so much wealth that I will be able to give to many more thousands of people and allow them to set themselves up to live their best lives in prosperity and happiness!

TIP

*No matter where you are on the financial scale; you always
have something to give, even if it is a dollar, a smile or helping
hand across the road.*

SHELLEY SYKES
THE HAPPINESS GURU

Start today you will feel happier for it!

I read a story in a book and I am not sure if it was the *One Minute Millionaire* or not, but it mentioned about doing something 'extraordinary' for someone, like paying for the toll charge for the car behind as a goodwill gesture. Well, I paused while reading the book and I put myself in the person's shoes. How would they feel to receive this unusually pleasant gesture? I began to laugh. I felt the emotion of surprise and joy, the appreciation and the goodwill. I knew then that the mere thought of receiving something so small yet unexpected, would bring a smile to that persons face all day!

I decided **to do such a gesture** the next time I was on a toll road. I never anticipated though, that it would impact so many people...

The tollbooth attendant was absolutely thrilled when I paid her for myself and the car behind...she couldn't wait to tell the lucky driver of the car...the driver papped his horn in appreciation. It was a man with an older lady in the passenger seat. She waved and grinned. He was so taken aback and so delighted; he paid for the car behind him!

How do I know? Well the tollbooth lady said **it continued like a ripple effect all day!** She, in her whole work experience had never experienced anything like it before. It had gone round the whole of the RTA Sydney Road traffic department! They were all talking about it at work and to their families at home...its surprising Merrick and Rosso from the Nova Radio Station hadn't got wind of it...they would have joined the queue!

The lesson – Once seen never forgotten! That may be true, but the joy of contribution is often worth its weight in gold.

Edward de Bono's comments

Balance

It must have become obvious by now that the problem of happiness is the problem of balance. This is a problem both of our perception and of our language because we prefer to deal with polarized situations and either/or decisions. Yet in the world of business and management the problem of balance has to be tackled in a definite manner. To make this easier the concepts of 'cut-off' and 'trade-off' have been developed. Cut-off implies that something may be worthwhile up to a point, but not beyond that point. So a hotel management may spend money on making a hotel more luxurious, but there is a cut off point beyond, which it is not worth spending more money. So pleasure may contribute to happiness up to a point, but beyond that point if may be counter productive and make happiness more difficult. Trade-off implies that one thing may have to be given up or 'traded' for another. A toy manufacturer would like to make his top more interesting, but the cost of manufacture would rise, so he has to exercise a trade-off between interest and cost. Similarly an individual may have consciously to exercise a trade-off between the need for excitement and peace. There is no reason why he should not base this on his experience or on how successful he is at either.

The problem of balance is also the problem of adjustment and change. How far does a person adjust himself to his situation and how far does he try to change his situation?

The answer to this problem has a major influence on happiness.

Shelley's comments

Sometimes we don't need a reason, just to give is enough to tip the scales in our favour for the balance to occur when we receive it equilibrates.

chapter 10

Happiness 24/7

 **TIP**

Pleasure in the present is the key.
Smooth and simple does it.

SHELLEY SYKES
THE HAPPINESS GURU

Many of the world's leading philosophers have produced a TV show or mini-movie called *'The Secret'*. They are all healthy, wealthy, happy and wise people.

(I don't know why Edward and I weren't invited to present our secret findings, perhaps we are going to be asked to present on the sequel). Anyway, these philosophers, business entrepreneurs, ordinary people that have achieved extraordinary things, all share the same secret! Their biggest wish now is to contribute to others by telling as many people as possible **the secret to be and stay healthy, wealthy, happy and wise.**

To summarise:

1. The Secret is we can 'all' have it all.
2. When we allow ourselves to dream big, the power of visualisation is the catalyst to creating our futures.

3. We can create what we visualise. When we believe anything is possible by trusting in the power of the universe, the impossible happens and our new realities are created according to our vision.
4. By just taking the first steps towards our dream lives, in supporting our beliefs and dreams, energy is transformed into physical matter.
5. The power of our words can make or break our dreams and desires whatever we say becomes our truth.
6. Passion is power.

Okay for some of you this resonates with you to the core, for some of you – this sounds too metaphysical for your liking and for your sakes I will simplify it.

Basically what ever we can dream, we can achieve and more.

If we think it is too hard it will be, however if we think 'anything is possible' – it is.

The easy part is you don't need to know how! Just 'go with the flow' and keep praying and ask for help, or keep asking someone or something for help every time you need it. Somehow if you are following your dreams your prayers get answered...sometimes bigger and brighter than you could ever expect and like in all good movies sometimes in ways you least expected.

Most financially rich people with a caring and happy disposition...and that is most wealthy people, like Ritchie Rich's Dad in the Walt Disney movie *'Ritchie Rich'* get this lesson in life earlier than some of us. Some never even get the lesson until next time around. Wouldn't it be great and it is possible, to have an abundant prosperous life. It brings one of my friends, John to tears every time he recounts the joy he gets from spreading the secret at his seminars. He is a man that experiences happiness and joy every day of his life. His message like Edward is about balance.

So to any of you who are still sceptical that happiness is a possibility every day of the year I say to you now – that if you CHOOSE to be HAPPY every day it, will become your reality. You will always find something to be grateful or joyous about. When good things are happening you will be grateful, because you have experienced the bad before. When bad things happen there is always balance in the universe and there will be something, someone, some dream that will bring a smile to your face, gladness from gratitude and the knowing that we have the power to change our present with the power of thought for our future.

Hollywood lifestyle here I come!!! Yeah Haa!
Can you call this fiction or fantasy? Who cares as long as it works!
As Edward says you can't lie about the future – it hasn't happened yet.
If, like having your own Genie, you can conjure up your own future would you go for mediocre or would you go for the choice of a dream life? The decision is always down to us. Remember we all deserve the best for us and the exciting thing is we all have different dreams.

Mine just keep getting bigger, brighter and more bubbly!

For those of you that need more practice to break old, less constructive habits, because you haven't been practicing this type of dream-creation and positive thinking as long as some of us, here are my 21 inspirational and motivational tips to keep you happy. They are split into 3 things to do in each of the 7 areas of life.

21 Inspirational & Motivational Tips for Happiness

Relationships

1. Be honest & Loving with yourself, best supporter not best critic
2. Be tolerant and focus on what **you can give** to the relationship
3. Be interested in them and listen more

Social

4. Be you and don't worry what others think – enjoy
5. Plan to do something at least once a week that you love doing socially
6. Contribute to someone's joy by making at least one person smile each day.

Career

7. Be you're best right now and shine at what ever you are doing right now
8. Look for the right opportunity to get you closer to your dream
9. Plan, review and congratulate yourself each week for your progress

Spirituality

10. Believe in yourself that you can be and do anything
11. Remind yourself you are not alone, you can ask for help
12. Be grateful for everything that's good right now

Health

13. Breath deeper daily
14. Drink more water daily
15. Tell yourself you are slim, trim & beautiful inside & out

Family & Friends

16. Love and leave them if they bring you down
17. Find friends that are more in line with the true you
18. Honest open communication – let it out from your heart

Financial

19. Find a mentor who's already there & where you're going
20. Take at least one action that will bring your dream closer
21. Revise your plan weekly & check how you are doing

According to my friend Robyn Pullman it takes 21 days to break bad habits. If you put into practice your happiness tips program I guarantee you will feel happy.

Edward de Bono's comments

Happiness is quite properly a vague and general word that needs no tight definition, since such a definition would add nothing to the understanding of it's meaning. If a person feels that they are happy, then they are happy. We can, however, look at some of the ingredients that from time to time are believed to contribute to happiness.

Pleasure is very real. There is the pleasure of friends, of beauty, of food, of drink, of humour, of achievement and of physical exercise. Pleasure is so real that we can insert an electrode into a rat's brain and stimulate the 'pleasure centre' directly and deliberately. One day we may be able to do this for man. In a way, with drugs we can almost do it now. It is this rather mechanical nature of pleasure, which has gotten it a bad reputation. Those religions that have sought to deny the self have done it on the basis that the self is naturally pleasure seeking and as a consequence greedy, selfish and self-indulgent. It is this excess of pleasure seeking, which has been seen as sinful and which has led to condemnation of any pleasure seeking.

The natural purpose of pleasure has been seen as the sugar coating on the pill to make man do the things that were necessary for survival as an organic system: food, drink, sex etc. Over indulgence in pleasure is rather like a child opening the bathroom cabinet and eating all the sweet tasting red iron pills, because of the sugar coating – and then suffering the very dangerous iron poisoning. If there was a natural cut off to pleasure – as there is to some extent in eating and drinking – there would be nothing to condemn. In the absence of a natural cut-off, man has to develop some sense of balance. It is towards the development of such a sense of balance that the new happy system is inclined rather than a condemnation of pleasure as such.

chapter 11

Live in Love & Gratitude

TIP

*Assume the colour of the rainbow in each person's perspective.
Things aren't just black or white there is grey and a whole
array of colours that are equally viable.
Respect their point of view, even if you don't agree,
they will love you for it.*

**SHELLEY SYKES
THE HAPPINESS GURU**

As we have said before people that are married live longer and on average have a much better health record than those living on their own?

When a woman had quadruplets, one of the babies was much smaller and weaker and the surgeons, who had had them in separate incubators couldn't do anything more to help them medically – a nurse on gut instinct, took the baby out of its incubator and placed it next to one of the other babies in their incubator. The result was amazing. The baby's vital signs picked up immediately and went from strength to strength.

Even an incubator is a large lonely place, when you're on your own and a premature baby. Your beautiful home or apartment can be lonely, when it is not shared. The sound of laughter or the movement of another person is comforting. Having someone there to talk to is uplifting.

My friends Chris and Brian have been happily married for nearly 20 years. They are one of my '**Lucky-in-Love**' friends. When Australia made the world cup, Brian and a few of his friends planned a trip to Europe to watch the games. It was the first time they had been away from one another for longer than a week. Chris was happy for Brian that he was going and like a big kid he set off with his Australian Team T-shirts, banners and scarves. It was a shock to Chris's system though when he had gone. The house seemed so quiet and empty despite having her daughter at home. She missed his presence and energy he brought to their home and the sharing, loving conversations, she had for so long taken for granted. She missed being able to just touch his strong arms and feel feminine and protected. Their bed seemed so much colder and bigger without him. It hit her hard – she suddenly became present and had an over whelming feeling of gratitude that this 'lonely empty feeling was for a short period of time.' She felt compassion for her single friends and had a clearer understanding of how they must feel. She filled up with gratitude that this was only a temporary situation for her, but made note that she would be more sympathetic and aware of their friends, that may need comfort or connection. Her feeling of happiness to know she had such a gorgeous man to love and be adored by, kept her joyous and focused on love and gratitude. The power of his presence and the positive contribution to their lives made a powerful impact. Well, as you can imagine he had the most gushy and heartfelt welcome home! He had a ball in Europe with his mates, but he was thrilled to be back to his loving family. The trust and love they have for one another allows them to be themselves and experience all of life's joys, yet the feeling of total acceptance and unconditional love is unbeatable.

This type of '**Lucky-in-Love**' scenario is what we all aim for. For those still on their journey towards their soul mate many choose to have pets that they can love, talk to and cuddle for this very reason.

We all know that some relationships can be more disruptive and negative to our lives than being on our own. Remembering nothing is right or wrong it just is, gives us the creative time to reflect what and whom we do want in our lives.

I used to believe attracting the right partner into our lives was tough and of course, what I focused on became my reality. As you know, I took it upon myself to investigate on behalf of all those *Sexy Singles and Ready To Mingles*, what the secret was for soul mate attraction and found that all the **Lucky-in-Loves** were being themselves and emitting magnetic vibrationary signals of high self-esteem and confidence. Their expectations for love were specific and like magnets, their ideal partners were equally balanced and attracted. It's worth getting a copy of my book '*Sexy Single and Ready to Mingle*' off my website www.shelleysykes.com just to validate where you are at in the cycle of things. 10% of the sale goes to charity and you will glean so much more on how to attract your soul mate or boost the passion in your existing relationship.

Spookily the 5-point formulae for loving lasting relationships works every time. Most **Sexy Singles** are in what I call the creative mode...creating their future selves with visualisation and positive belief. According to 'The Secret's' philosophers if the **Sexy Singles** start to doubt ever meeting their ideal partners then 'puff' like magic their new negative belief, becomes their new possibility and repels the soul mate or they disappear in a puff of smoke completely like magic. Recognise the yoyo signs and wonder why you are gorgeous and still alone?

If however **Sexy Singles** go about their business expecting to have fun, pleasure and to meet their mate at the right time for them, in the right way as all **Lucky-in-Loves** say, magic happens when you least expect it and their partners are just like or better than they imagined their ideal soul mate would be!

Forgiveness

Many times our experiences can have us doubting ourselves and that has to be overcome. Forgiveness to others is the best medicine. I know many women who hold grudges and it affects them physically, often getting cancer, they become grouchy and lack joy and they zap other peoples energy levels – which if they have children can be very detrimental to the kids, because they can't walk away. Forgiveness is the quickest way to fast track your life.

Responsibility

It is up to all of us to take responsibility for our own creations and experiences in life. It is far more empowering than feeling as if we have no control when we have designed our life the way it is, earlier in our past. It is even scarier knowing however, that we have the power to change our lifestyle and future with visualisation and yet many don't, they keep duplicating the same old, same old and wonder why they are depressed with the sameness of their lives. Taking responsibility for everything happening in your life is the second fastest track to health, wealth and happiness.

In it for the long haul

Some people enjoy the excitement of the chase, the not knowing does she or doesn't he and when a relaxed balanced relationship starts to form they seek more excitement. People at this stage in their lives are only creating for the short term and fear lack and loss. The grass is always greener syndrome. If you know that you have the power to create a long, lasting, loving, passionate relationship that gets better and better every year, would you want to keep swapping?

Remembering nothing is wrong or right . . . living with love in your heart and being grateful for the beautiful people you are meeting is enough to keep the happiness dial switched on and in balance.

Edward de Bono's comments

Excitement, like pleasure, is another danger area.

Novelty soon wears off and the seeking of excitement demands more and more effort. The search for stimulation and novelty gets more difficult. The periods between the excitements grow ever more boring. Boredom is created by excitement, not by the lack of it. It is the hankering for excitement, the memory of it and the troughs between peaks of excitement that create boredom. A country dweller that becomes acquainted with the excitements of the town can now develop boredom towards the country. Excitement creates boredom as surely as pleasure creates indigestion. What is the alternative? Should we eschew excitement in favour of a life of tranquil peace and contentment, relying on developed sensitivities to provide pleasure? It is fair to argue that pleasure and excitement are actually counter-productive, because they blunt the senses and so make it more and more difficult to achieve the same effect. It is quite impossible to recapture the thrill of driving a motorcar on one's own for the first time, or having one's first book published. The first kiss of a romance is always the best. Is it possible to sensitise the mind so that the arrival of any stranger at a remote country farm, becomes as exciting as the part of the century for a socialite?

To be aware of possibilities that go beyond the usual routine enlarges life. Not all new things are good. But opportunities for increasing sensibilities are usually good. You can always drop them if they prove otherwise.

chapter 12

Fake It till you Make It

TIP

*If anything is possible,
why not go for the possibilities you dream up?
For what you can dream, you can achieve.
It isn't a lie to predict something in the future, because how
can you lie about something that hasn't happened yet!*

**SHELLEY SYKES
THE HAPPINESS GURU**

When I have clients, who are doing jobs that they don't like, I always ask them 'what is your dream vocation? If I had a magic wand, what would you absolutely love to do?' One of my clients John 'was' a teacher. I could tell he was stressed with tell tale signs of psoriasis on his face and hands. He was having his Vitamin and Mineral body check at one of my Forever Young Clinics, because he felt 'exhausted' most of the time and of course his skin condition was uncomfortable and unsightly at times. Predictably he was deficient in many vitamins and minerals, which was affecting his body functionality. When posed with my question 'what is your dream profession' his energy monitor rocketed and with a wide smile he said it was his dream to be a singer. His whole body lifted from its curved lumped position and my Din Y San machine registered a higher body energy reading! The transformation was instant.

So that is when we came up with the saying, when asked 'what do you do?' His response was to be "I'm a singer and I teach in between performances!"

John's face was a picture. He positively glowed. He just couldn't stop smiling and I am sure his psoriasis started to look less red and inflamed from that instant. I even got him to sing to me in the clinic! He has a wonderful voice.

True to form, John is in great health now. His vitamin and mineral levels are all normal and as a result the psoriasis has 'disappeared.' Every now and then I ask John – what do you do? And he just laughs and says, I'm a singer and I teach at the college in between performances.' He has joined the amateur dramatic society and he sings at the old peoples homes to practice his new repertoire of songs. Life is GREAT. He is happy and spreading joy to his students at school, the old people and his audiences!

Lady in Red – Romance Despite Social Standing

Most people have seen the romantic movie *Pretty Woman* with Julia Roberts, who at the beginning of the movie is introduced as a 'hooker' or lady of the street. However when multi-millionaire, the good looking Richard Gere takes her under his wing with training and encouragement, she transforms into an elegant, sincere lady, loved and liked by all. She didn't suddenly become the 'lady' she had to 'learn' her role.

- She had to dress like a groomed lady...
- Be beautified and groomed.
- Taught deportment.
- Learn etiquette and table manners.
- How to be comfortable in social settings – decorum

All these traits are learnable, yet what was the most wonderful asset that isn't so learnable was her beautiful, fun loving natural personality and spirit. She had a heart of gold and a humbleness, which was charming – and **that** was what attracted the gorgeous Richard Gere to her. He could teach her how to be a lady, but you can't teach passion and put the spirit into the lady! That comes from the inside. Julia wanted to learn, she wanted to be 'the princess' yet stay true to her beautiful character and that is truly what we all could associate with her. The happy ending story didn't come at a price of changing her spirit.

It shows us that despite our humble beginnings that we can all become, what ever we want to be despite our past.

My Fair Lady – Elocution lessons

In the movie *My Fair Lady* a similar theme happens there. Professor Higgins decides to test the theory to see if he can 'make a lady' of Eliza Doolittle. Until she has the desire 'to want to become a lady' and speak and dress like one – it is an uphill struggle for the professor. Then she gets the motivation – she falls in love and wants to be in the world of the professor and be posh. Her passion and desire are ignited and she becomes posher than the posh people!

Nobody can make you be and do anything you don't want to be or do effectively. We need to have the desire and passion to be great at it.

Educating Rita – self-improvement

In this movie Rita is a hairdresser, but secretly she had always wanted to go to college and become educated. She finally decides to take action by registering into college.

Go Girl! We all have to take action for the universe and creation to manifest the new life we dream of.

Rita feels empowered by going to college. She is over awed and feels so much 'less' than the other students though (her perception, not theirs) and at times wonders 'who does she think she is?' She felt a 'fake.' She felt like college was for only very smart, young students. It was her perception at that down moment. College is for all people to learn something new. She was a student and every day she was learning something new – so she really was a very good enthusiastic student. The desire to learn was so great she perseveres, like all successful people they never quit.

Unlike the previous two movie stories Rita's teacher Michael Caine is a burnt out alcoholic, who has given up on his passion and dreams. He really doesn't care and has lost his desire, because one of his published books was rejected. Should that have stopped him writing? No. Other people's opinion is not his business. Rita's desire and enthusiasm for literature reignites his flame to get back onto his track and follow his career as a writer and be a 'great inspirational teacher.'

*We can all be and do what ever we want to be, do or become.
We have to almost be, do and become whatever we want to
be, do or become first though before we actually become it!
You could call this faking it until you make it —
yet in the true sense it is just moving into being.*

**SHELLEY SYKES
THE HAPPINESS GURU**

The young princes of England are groomed and trained to 'be princes.' They are born of royal blood, but really start out like everyone, just as young boys. Mary from Tasmania has 'turned into a beautiful Danish princess.' She has had to work very hard at it, learning to speak the language fluently, how to dress, how to handle international dignitaries, be gracious to family members and people she doesn't like or know. Her love of her prince and baby are all there. She is still the Australian girl that has a new life.

Bono the singer when he was a boy probably always dreamt of being a rock star and his dreams and desires and actions transformed him into a rock legend with a great heart and soul.

Edward de Bono's comments

Perception

Perception is a pattern-making process, as we have seen in a previous section. Its initial patterns would trap the mind forever unless it had the ability suddenly to switch over and see things in a different way. This is the basis of insight, creativity, learning and progress. It is the aim of the techniques of lateral thinking and **The Happiness Bug**. This pattern-switching ability is vital to a patterning system, which simply could not work without it. And humour is the most direct and obvious expression of this pattern-switching ability. We suddenly see something in a new way, and we laugh. Because humour is so enjoyable and so easy and so apparently trivial we tend to overlook just how fundamental a process it is to the human mind. It has always surprised me how little attention philosophers have paid to humour since it is a more significant process of mind than is reason. Reason can only sort out perceptions, but the humour process is involved in changing them.

Because humour is the outward expression of this pattern switching process it symbolises such things as possibility, hope, change, creativeness, new ways of looking at things, evolution and ultimately a happier state.

chapter 13

Cure or Contaminate

 **TIP**

*Like Light our loving thoughts ripple out
and touch those around us.
The happiness we share also ripples out and
contaminates those we touch with our love & laughter.*

**SHELLEY SYKES
THE HAPPINESS GURU**

Some of you may be thinking, who would want to be 'cured from feeling happy every day', but there are those people that actually enjoy and feel significant wallowing in their misery and ill health, bad behaviour or cantankerousness.

They get attention from their negative anti-social behaviour. I know living with a teenager can sometimes be like living with Darth Vader from the dark side. They need attention, but seem to get it all for the wrong reasons and in the most negative and draining way. What happened to our sweet angels? Don't they want a happy easy life?

Energy is energy as my friend Rik says, it is always 100%, and it just changes form. Some people gain significance from being the sick person, some from being the bully, while others by 'doing the right thing' or pleasing as many people as they can.

As Ron Hubbard states human's first primary focus is survival. We all want to survive and his definition of success is the degree by which survival becomes pleasurable. The more pleasurable survival is for you the more successful you are as a human.

Another definition of success is living the way you want to live and enjoying the journey. We have mentioned in the previous chapter how our perceptions can make success easy to come by or hard.

What every parent wants for their children is for them to be happy – to be healthly, wealthly and learn from their elders the easy way rather than making every mistake in the book. I learnt very early on, that the goals I set my son weren't the goals that inspired him. He had his own agenda. By 4½ years young he was still not able to walk without callipers and a walking frame and I presumed his biggest wish was to learn to walk . . . "No" he said "I'm not bothered about walking . . . I want to learn to run like Forest Gump and have my leg-irons smash into millions of pieces so that I can run like the wind!"
Well that was that. I crossed off 'walking' and inspired him with the carrot he himself gave me. I said that the week he took his first step alone I would fly us both to Disney World to buy some Lion King running shoes and meet Tiger and Pooh. It took only 2 weeks and we were jetting across the Atlantic for the Lion King running shoes!

He ran his first race with a lead start at the age of 6 and I was the proudest mum shouting "Run Callum! Run!" Just like the girl in his favourite movie. He came last, but he now could run with the running shoes to prove it!

The power we have is amazing if we realise what it is that turns us on.

Nelson Mandela says that our biggest fear is not to speak in public, but to shine our light. We are often fearful of our own brilliance and power.

I personally believe that the only way we can survive mentally, physically and spiritually is not the degree of comfort, but the degree to which we know ourselves and follow our own hearts desire, no matter what that is.

No one can give you your passion, drive and purpose. Only you will truly know that and you find it by listening to your inner voice and travelling the road of least resistance.

Tiger Woods doesn't try to improve the worst swing – no he focuses on all the swings he can easily do and enjoys doing so that he never has to use the swing he is poor at! Why do it tough?

The Happiness Bug allows people to feel the joy and put themselves first and do what it takes to, as Anthony Robbins says unleash our power. Why would we want to be cured from that?

We all know that if a person laughs and then laughs a bit more, we all start to laugh along and often we have no idea why?

Laughter is contagious just like a wonderful smile. You've tried looking at your self in the mirror with a smile on your face, you actually beam wider on seeing your own happy face. We are wired for happiness. As humans we are a form of energy that can be measured in MegaHertz or vibrations. High energy keeps germs and nasty bugs away. Yet thankfully high energy attracts **The Happiness Bug** – scientifically proven that happy people have a higher vibration and a healthier happier outlook filled with more joy than sorrow.

My friend Dave Rogers has just sent an email with a news letter he is posting in a magazine, just as I am typing this last section of the book – I was surprised as always at the synchronicity, the content and timing of such a message, which I have copied as was sent to me now!

His article is called:

7 ESSENTIALS TO LIVE A VIBRANT LIFE

In the past twelve months, my path has crossed with some masters of health and wellness. Each of these individuals work with people to shift them from a reality of illness, dis-ease, and even cancer to a reality of vibrancy, energy, love and light.

#7 Malaysia Chi Kong Master SK smiled at me and shared that a resourceful state is deeply connected to breathing. He strongly urged people with any illness to breath in light, life and energy and breath out waste, discharge and un-resourceful thoughts.

Focused healthy breathing for at least 30 minutes a day will prepare the body to secrete and release natural healing endorphins.

#6 Paul Kirk, former cancer patient and now a health and wellness consultant in New Zealand, suggests that water must be a major component of the healthy life plan. Energise the water with positive thoughts and drink clean, mineralised water, at least eight to ten glassed a day is a must suggests Kirk.

#5 Kirk continues that exercise is something that every well person should incorporate into his or her lifestyle. If your body is suffering from some dis-ease, he says, "Fine start exercising, perhaps some simple walking, stretching, and movements to get the body moving."

#4 Sunlight is a key to your recovery from cancer suggests author and health revolutionary Don Tolman.

#3 Author Tolman demonstrates in his whole food encyclopedias that whole foods, fresh fruit, nuts, and vegetables are an essential key in giving your body a chance to recover, replenish and restock vitamins and minerals to shift you to a healthy and vibrant state.

#2 Dr George, an ayuhvedic practioner & personal friend, adds that personal prayer or mediation is a wonderful antioxidant for people's diseases. Dr George suggests at least 30 minutes a day for individual or group prayer or mediation as a wonderful source of centeredness and certainly of health recovery.

#1 The Happiness Guru Shelley Sykes has documented numerous examples of laughter being utilised to shift people into a resourceful state of happiness, wellness and vibrancy.

As part of this very special remedy for dis-ease, put it to practice, see if it works for you and see if you can influence your health and wellness most!

Love Dave

Here is a well travelled man meeting and infecting people of influence and who all confirm we have the control and power to heal and be happy

Your Journey onwards & upwards

 **TIP**

Fun = (Happiness + Love) × Adventure

SHELLEY SYKES
THE HAPPINESS GURU

Remember there are no right ways or wrong ways, just enjoy your journey of discovery and make it a pleasure for yourselves and those around you spreading your happiness where you can so that we can all love in contaminated bliss.

May all your wishes and dreams come true,
Love and laughter,

Shelley

Edward de Bono's comments

There is the achievement of performance as well as the achievement of destination. The achievement of performance is more important and more surely a means to happiness. Achievement is the definition of the self in action. Life itself is the achievement of a self-organising system, and living is its achievement of performance. Achievement is personal and is to be carefully distinguished from the image of high achievement pressure and the competitive need. A carpenter is a more successful achiever than a politician.

chapter 14

Happy
Quick Fix It Tips

Here are lists of the useful motivational, inspirational tips you can refer to that I have highlighted throughout the book to keep you lifted and focused...

TIP

*We can each be a 'powerful magnet'
Often referred to as our personal power or magnetism.*

SHELLEY SYKES

THE HAPPINESS GURU

TIP

*Confidence and expectancy
are essential to our success*

SHELLEY SYKES

THE HAPPINESS GURU

TIP

Magic happens despite our circumstances!

SHELLEY SYKES

THE HAPPINESS GURU

 **TIP**

Nothing is ever wrong. It just is.

SHELLEY SYKES

THE HAPPINESS GURU

 **TIP**

*Reality all depends on the **meaning we give things** and the 'barriers' we surround ourselves with and not because there is anything 'wrong' with us or the situation. It is down to us and our own perceptions.*

SHELLEY SYKES

THE HAPPINESS GURU

 **TIP**

Love yourself first and work out how you can be the best you can be.

SHELLEY SYKES

THE HAPPINESS GURU

 **TIP**

*My new belief is that **we are all just perfect as we are right now**. We don't need to **'change anything about ourselves'**, but instead perhaps just push down a few barriers we ourselves have propped up, because of the meaning we have given situations and events that have happened to us in the past.*

SHELLEY SYKES

THE HAPPINESS GURU

 **TIP**

Many of us don't realise how special we are.
*We all **DESERVE** to be **truly loved**.*
*We can choose a **happy state** for ourselves.*
*We are all **beautiful inside** and **out**.*

SHELLEY SYKES

THE HAPPINESS GURU

 **TIP**

Assume the colour of the rainbow in each person's perspective.
Things aren't just black or white there is grey and a whole
array of colours that are equally viable. Respect their point of
view even if you don't agree they will love you for it.

SHELLEY SYKES

THE HAPPINESS GURU

 **TIP**

If we feel healthy, happy and well then we attract
people to us like moths to a flame!
JUST THE RESULT WE ARE WANTING!

SHELLEY SYKES

THE HAPPINESS GURU

TIP

Attitude and passion are everything!

SHELLEY SYKES

THE HAPPINESS GURU

TIP

*There is nothing wrong with us, or our up bringing.
There will have been other benefits of being raised
the way we were raised. It just is!*

SHELLEY SYKES

THE HAPPINESS GURU

TIP

*We only need to role model those that are 'happily' and
'passionately' in love with a fun 'joie de vive!'*

SHELLEY SYKES

THE HAPPINESS GURU

TIP

*Always honour and respect yourself first and do the right thing
by yourself. You will have no regrets that way and
feel more empowered.*

SHELLEY SYKES

THE HAPPINESS GURU

TIP

*Freedom of love expands not withers. Love and let go. If it's
meant to be it will return ten fold.*

SHELLEY SYKES

THE HAPPINESS GURU

 **TIP**

To be courageous is to fear, but still take action any way!

SHELLEY SYKES

THE HAPPINESS GURU

 **TIP**

The more in tune we are about being our authentic selves and not worrying about what others think, the stronger our magnet draws like people towards us.

SHELLEY SYKES

THE HAPPINESS GURU

 **TIP**

We are ALL 2mm away from finding our Soul mates! Turn around they may be standing behind you.

SHELLEY SYKES

THE HAPPINESS GURU

TIP

If we create the possibility for ourselves there are plenty of souls for us to attract and not in scarce supply, panic and desperation is lifted from our demeanour.

SHELLEY SYKES

THE HAPPINESS GURU

TIP

*Live in **gratitude** and decide it is a must to choose to have **a happy attitude**.*

SHELLEY SYKES

THE HAPPINESS GURU

TIP

If we haven't yet found our soul mate then nothing is wrong — everything is perfect. We are just taking stepping-stones on our journey to be with our true love.

SHELLEY SYKES

THE HAPPINESS GURU

TIP

*The '**Lucky-in-Loves**'© didn't know how, when or where they were going to meet, they just 'expected' it to happen! Often they say it 'happened' when they least expected it to happen — but it happened.*

SHELLEY SYKES

THE HAPPINESS GURU

TIP

Opposites don't always have the best sustainable relationships.

SHELLEY SYKES

THE HAPPINESS GURU

TIP

We need to be in state! A happy state – a state that we choose to have despite our circumstances by focusing on what is RIGHT in our lives.
We need to communicate honestly with ourselves and others.
We need to love ourselves and look after our health.
We need to trust and know that we are enough.

SHELLEY SYKES

THE HAPPINESS GURU

TIP

All is well. All is well.

SHELLEY SYKES

THE HAPPINESS GURU

TIP

*My belief is that an **ideal relationship** is where two people that come together become **even stronger as a team** than as individuals.*

SHELLEY SYKES

THE HAPPINESS GURU

TIP

We can be whatever we decide we want to be.

SHELLEY SYKES

THE HAPPINESS GURU

TIP

*The more in tune we are about being our authentic selves
and not worrying about what others think,
the stronger our magnet draws like people towards us.*

SHELLEY SYKES

THE HAPPINESS GURU

TIP

*Be strong in the 7 key areas of life
so that we attract our equal and not our antithesis —
Spirituality, Relationships, Career, Family and Friends,
Wealth, Interests, Health.*

SHELLEY SYKES

THE HAPPINESS GURU

TIP

Wealth is certainly in the air and can be created or manifested!

SHELLEY SYKES

THE HAPPINESS GURU

TIP

*It makes sense for a happy person to choose to be with another
happy person…it's easier and they can be even happier
spreading more ripples of happiness around them.*

SHELLEY SYKES

THE HAPPINESS GURU

TIP

*Select friends and relationships that are your type of people
that you can respect and admire.*

SHELLEY SYKES

THE HAPPINESS GURU

TIP

*Dream about your ideal soul mate in every facet – looks,
behaviour, how they treat you, type of work they do, interests,
financial status, where they live, do they love kids,
spirituality . . .*

SHELLEY SYKES

THE HAPPINESS GURU

TIP

*We **Sexy Singles** need to realise that we are all
at the right place at the right time.
We are potential '**Lucky-in-Loves**' preparing to happen.*

SHELLEY SYKES

THE HAPPINESS GURU

TIP

*Dream your dream and take action to get there.
Never ever quit.*

SHELLEY SYKES

THE HAPPINESS GURU

TIP

Remember nothing is wrong.
Love is our right and to live in love is our possibility according to
the Bible, Koran…and all the religious teachings of the world.
It is the one thing every religion agrees upon.

SHELLEY SYKES

THE HAPPINESS GURU

TIP

*Don't ever try and "**help**" your partner be different*
They either are or aren't that way
whichever way you want them to be

SHELLEY SYKES

THE HAPPINESS GURU

TIP

Everyone is different but in general terms I reckon a woman
wants a man that has honest communication, respects her,
listens, spoils and supports her…romances her and ultimately
is her best friend.

SHELLEY SYKES

THE HAPPINESS GURU

TIP

Choose to be connected and in the flow.

SHELLEY SYKES

THE HAPPINESS GURU

TIP

*If we come from the possibility that **nothing is wrong**
and every experience is a **lesson**, then we can relax a little
and begin to enjoy the outcomes of our actions good or bad.
We can apply lateral thinking and create new realms
of how we want our future to be.*

SHELLEY SYKES

THE HAPPINESS GURU

TIP

*People say and do bad things – it's a fact.
We don't have to take them as our truth.*

SHELLEY SYKES

THE HAPPINESS GURU

TIP

*When a relationship doesn't last…don't get sad.
Be thankful because that one obviously was a stepping-stone.
Get excited that the next one is going to be even more lovable
and exciting!*

SHELLEY SYKES

THE HAPPINESS GURU

TIP

It's our duty to stay kissable for everyone!

SHELLEY SYKES

THE HAPPINESS GURU

 **TIP**

Forgiving and Making up can be the most passionate and liberating feeling a couple can gift to one another. Be compassionate and keep the love and respect burning!

SHELLEY SYKES

THE HAPPINESS GURU

TIP

Health, Beauty and Style have always gone hand in hand in my opinion and you need the Wealth to pay for it!

SHELLEY SYKES

THE HAPPINESS GURU

TIP

*We always have a choice. We can choose to accept others criticisms or not. **Not** is preferable.*

SHELLEY SYKES

THE HAPPINESS GURU

TIP

It isn't what happens to you in life that counts, it's what you do about it that matters.

W. MITCHELL AND RORY SYKES

TIP

Love is...

Talking, listening, eye contact – feeling fascinated, happy and interested, more affectionate!

SHELLEY SYKES

THE HAPPINESS GURU

TIP

As a slim 'Sexy Single & Ready to Mingle' girl I found the secret to being slim was breathing more deeply, that water in – meant weight off and keeping slim was mind over matter... think thin and you'll become what you think!

SHELLEY SYKES

THE HAPPINESS GURU

TIP

The real fact is that whatever your particular requirements are, there is probably someone out there that has those qualities just stay true to what you truly want.

SHELLEY SYKES

THE HAPPINESS GURU

TIP

Choose to respect and honour those around you. Truly listen to them and stay present.

SHELLEY SYKES

THE HAPPINESS GURU

TIP

The more in tune we are about being our authentic selves and not worrying about what others think, the stronger our magnet draws like people towards us.

SHELLEY SYKES

THE HAPPINESS GURU

TIP

Respect of anyone is a great value. Respect in a long-term relationship is what keeps that relationship united.

SHELLEY SYKES

THE HAPPINESS GURU

TIP

Sex-ercise for your soul regularly for your health and well-being.

SHELLEY SYKES

THE HAPPINESS GURU

TIP

Look at what is right in your life. It will bring a smile to your face.

SHELLEY SYKES

THE HAPPINESS GURU

TIP

Happiness is...
Having eyes to see the scenery,
Ears to hear the sounds of music,
Noses to smell the freshness of cooked food.

SHELLEY SYKES

THE HAPPINESS GURU

TIP

Happiness is...
Having the choice to make decisions.
Freedom is fabulous! Enjoy!

SHELLEY SYKES

THE HAPPINESS GURU

TIP

Happiness is...
Following the path of least resistance.
Go with the flow.

SHELLEY SYKES

THE HAPPINESS GURU

TIP

Happiness is...
Living in love with yourself and others.
You are gorgeous, no matter what!

SHELLEY SYKES

THE HAPPINESS GURU

 **TIP**

*Communication to me, is about giving out a message
that can be understood and that the
message sent is perceived that way it was intended
to bring pleasure, love and respect.*

SHELLEY SYKES

THE HAPPINESS GURU

TIP

$FUN = (Happiness + Love) \times Adventure$

SHELLEY SYKES

THE HAPPINESS GURU

Happiness is easy to catch, very contagious and so much fun...remember when you were little and you played doctor and nurses, well this game is even better! Have fun trying it out for size.

Just always be gentle on yourself...you are like an orchid, beautiful, vibrant, but you can go limp if you don't have enough sunshine and plenty of water!

Spoil yourselves often.

Love and laughter...the queen of butterflies

The Happiness Bug

Shelley's ABC for happiness...

Always shine your light
Be the best you can be
Count your blessings
Dream big
Expect magic to happen despite your circumstances
Follow your intuition
Get up and go
Have fun
Imagine and create your own reality
Judge no one
Know what you want
Live in gratitude
Mean what you say and honour your word
Never lose hope
Open your heart and let love in
Passion is possible
Quiet time allows you to create
Remember life is a journey
Stay true to whom you are
Treat others with respect
Understand nothing is wrong. It just is
Visualise what you really want
Win – win there are no losers
X-ercise
You are beautiful inside and out
Zz spend more time in bed

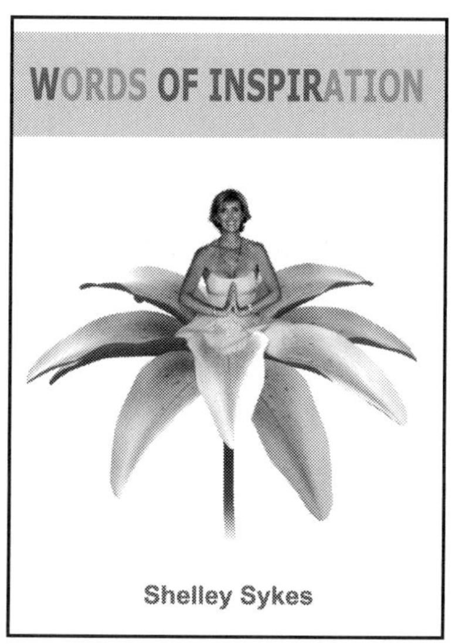

Words of inspiration is a book filled with daily quotes and a call to action, that will inspire you to follow your own dreams and passions. It can be read sequentially or at random. You always get the right message at the right time!

www.shelleysykes.com

Price: $24.95

Happiness Experience Seminars

Shelley will be conducting seminars around the world to teach the **Happiness Experience** techniques to all those that wish to be able to keep the **Happiness Syndrome** alive and well each day.

Become empowered and make every moment count.

Happiness is an attitude and if you would like to have **The Happiness Experience** each day to achieve your dreams and live your best lives then this seminar is not to be missed.

Ideal for leadership
Presentation Skills
Inter-personal communication skills
Positive Attitude
Personal Development

Book now.

www.shelleysykes.com

Happy Energising Spray

$24.95

www.shelleysykes.com

Happy Energising Spray

Need a little help to lift your mood?

Happy Energising Spray will lift those blues and make you bounce.

Happy Energising Spray is scientifcally proven to raise your vibration. Take the pressure out of concentrated effort, let the essential oils and nutrients lift your aura the natural way, effective immediately.

Price: $24.95

www.shelleysykes.com

Happiness Bug
T-Shirts

You can purchase on line any of the following T-shirts:

- Beware Happiness is contagious
- I'm Happy
- I've caught the Happiness Bug (No logo)
- I've caught the Happiness Bug (lge logo)
- I've caught the Happiness Bug (sml logo)
- I've caught the Happiness Bug (centre logo)
- Happy
- Get Syked
- I'm Syked

Colours: Black/White or Pink
Sizes: Small, Medium, Large & Extra Large
Price: $35

www.shelleysykes.com

I've caught the
Happiness Bug

Beware
Beware
Happiness is contagious
Beware
ware

HAPPY
HAPPY
HAPPY
HAPPY

I'm Syked
S
y
k
e
d

Get Syked

I've caught the
Happiness Bug

I've caught the
Happiness Bug

I'm
HAPPY

I've caught the
Happiness Bug

$495.00

www.shelleysykes.com.au

Health, Wealth & Happiness DVD's

No time to re-read the book but want some revision?

What better way than to be entertained, whilst you learn from ordinary people doing extraordinary things and achieving impossibilities?

Watch and learn with your own set of DVD's...

 Dream and Achieve

 Style and Image

 Wealth Creation

 Goals and Beliefs

 Health and Happiness

5 DVD's with hours of interviews and hundreds of tips from Celebrities, Olympic Champions, Gurus such as Edward de Bono and Siimon Reynolds and many more inspirational people living their dream lives and teaching you the tips and tools to make it yourself.

Order it NOW from **www.shelleysykes.com**

All inclusive special deal for readers $495.00

The Happiness Bug

'Magic happens despite
your circumstances.
It isn't what happens
to you in life that counts.
It's what you do about it
that matters!'

SHELLEY SYKES

www.shelleysykes.com

The Happiness Bug

'A happy person is a
fulfilled person'

EDWARD DE BONO

www.shelleysykes.com

Happiness Association

You qualify as a reader and generally gorgeous person to join the **Association of Happiness**.

This is a unique membership for people who have caught **'The Happiness Bug'** and are now contaminating others with their Happiness Syndrome.

You will be invited to global and local events that increase your circle of contacts, whilst having fun with other happy people. You will be an inspiration to those still wishing to be happy. To register please logon to:

www.shelleysykes.com

You will also be eligible for a FREE Newsletter and future notice of books, magazines, seminars and shows.

Forever Young

Forever Young,
I want to be Forever Young
Do you really want to live forever,
forever and ever

Youth Group

Forever Young

Allergy and Anti-Aging Clinics

TOTAL WELLNESS PACKAGE
Includes All 3 Treatments
Normally $390
Special Price only **$300**

1 
Vitamin Screening
88 Vitamin & Mineral Tests

2 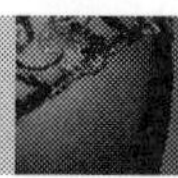
Cellulite Removal
or Remedial Body Massage

3 
Forever Young Anti-Aging
4-in-1 Facial

Book Now: +61 438 016 622
For Your Forever Young Total Wellness Package

Feel Energised, **Get** Slimmer
Look Forever Young

Clinics:

North Ryde	Double Bay	Mosman
Specialist Medical Centre	Shop 11, The Promenade	The Medical Centre
1st Floor, 124a Epping Road	The Stamford Plaza, 33 Cross Street	Military Road
North Ryde, NSW 2113	Double Bay, NSW 2128	Mosman, NSW 2088

For Franchising Information Please Visit:
www.foreveryoungclinics.com

Get Syked –
Style Seminars

For those of you interested in learning the art of pampering yourself and bringing your personality and creating your image to suit the person you are creating, then book to be on one of Shelley's popular style seminars.

1. Learn how to brand yourself and create a non-verbal message.
2. From 'Hats to Heels' and every occasion gain the skills that give you self-esteem and confidence.
3. Heaps of beauty and health tips.
4. Learn how to put your style and personality into your home and reflect the you that you have created and are developing into.

Log onto www.shelleysykes.com

View the tips and tools and get a free newsletter:

www.beautifulunlimited.com

Relationship Seminars

Shelley Sykes is a sought after Inspirational Speaker as well as an author and TV Presenter. Her audience laugh and learn about love, luck, looks and lifestyle. She is based in Sydney, yet she speaks around the world at Relationship seminars.

Need a little love in your life?
Take action and become a passionate partner or soul mate magnet.

If you want to organise an event or sponsor Shelley to present her relationship seminars for your company then please contact:

Shelley Sykes
PO Box 452
Concord
Sydney NSW
Australia
T: +61 438 016622
shelley@shelleysykes.com

I'm
Sexy, Single & Ready
to Mingle

I'm
Sexy & Single

I was Sexy & Single
Now I'm
Lucky-in-Love

Lucky-in-Love...and
still Sexy!

I'm a
Chick Magnet!

I'm a
Man Magnet!

Beware
Beware
I'M SEXY!
eware
beware
re
ware

SEXY &
SINGLE

Beware
Beware
I'M SEXY!
eware
Beware
re
ware

Sexy Single
T-Shirts

You can purchase on line any of the following T-shirts:

- I'm Sexy, Single & Ready to Mingle
- I'm Sexy & Single
- I was Sexy & Single Now I'm **Lucky-in-Love**
- **Lucky-in-Love** . . . and still Sexy
- I'm a Chick Magnet!
- I'm a Man Magnet!
- Beware I'm Sexy
- Large logo – Sexy & Single

Colours: Black/White or Pink
Sizes: Small, Medium, Large & Extra Large
Price: $35

www.shelleysykes.com

I'm Sexy Single & I'm ready to Mingle
My mind's made up,
And my body's a tingle
Edward de Bono says love is a must
Don't be a Bridgette Jones
Brush off the dust...

Shelley Sykes

Happiness is . . . a loving relationship

Why not give a dating agency a go such as **RSVP it's FREE!**

Or if you have a high profile position and discretion is most important and you don't want anyone knowing your business, then the up market but more expensive option is **Connect4Love.** They specialise in match-making for the busy high flyers, celebrity, CEO's and millionaires with a fabulous, very confidential service, which includes the organising of restaurants, limousines, flower services, gift services, helicopter flights, weekend getaways and surprise cocktail parties . . .

They guarantee discretion and very personal service. Prices range from $1000 to $10,000 – worth it if you find your ideal partner!

Corporate Consultancy

Shelley is commissioned to work in a consultancy capacity to support your leadership teams to create and continue Happy Relations at work.

- For reduced staff turnover
- Increased profits
- Happier work environments

For further details contact: shelley@shelleysykes.com

2B1 Charitable Foundation

If you want to make an active contribution on your journey to faster and greater joy and prosperity...as well as **Make a Difference** log onto

www.2b1charity.org

You can become a regular supporter of our local and international projects such as:

Dolphcomm – sponsoring children and adults with needs to swim with wild dolphins

Step to the Future – teenager leadership skills.

Worldwide Food Organisation – teaching people in starved lands how to become self-sufficient.

Plant a Tree – Helping replenish the trees.

2B1 Charitable Foundation – Global One Hour of Happiness Day Challenge to start on 07/07/07.

Wannabee foundation – helping children.

One world – One Planet – One People – 2B1

2B1 Charitable Foundation, PO Box 452, Concord, NSW, 2137, Australia

Books by Shelley Sykes

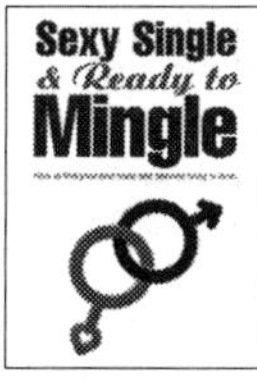

Sexy Single & Ready to Mingle

This is a recipe for relationships. How to magnetise your soul mate into your life to become **Lucky-in-Loves**. Edward de Bono calls it the Karma Sutra of the mind. $24.95

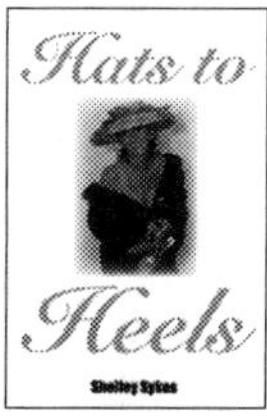

Hats to Heels

How to dress to impress!

Learn how to get the 'look' – Personal Branding at its best to suit your lifestyle and personality.

Vogue magazines calls this book a winner! $24.95

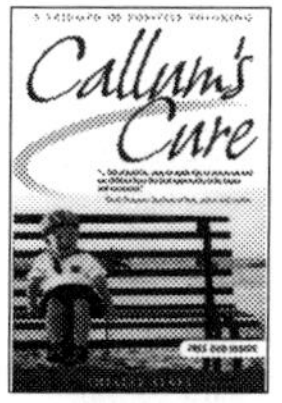

Callum's Cure

Inspirational true life story of Shelley and her quest to be the best person and parent.

Best-seller $24.95

Words of Inspiration

The Happiness Guru has summated all her tips into one book with call to action. This book can be used daily. $24.95

Coming soon . . . Forever Young & The Road to Wealth.

10% all book sales goes to the 2B1 Charitable Foundation.

www.shelleysykes.com

About Shelley Sykes

Born on her mother's birthday on 29th July in Yorkshire – Shelley grew up dreaming of becoming a doctor.

However at 19 years old, she emigrated to South Africa on her own to persue her studies and career in IT and the corporate world of banking, before experiencing life in the Travel, Hospitality and Entertainment industries.

After 7 wonderful years, she moved on to live in Malawi, then Crete, as a PR and United Nations Hostess for a couple of years and back to the UK, where she met her first husband. A fairytale marriage in Acapulco ensued, but divorced after their only child was born with Cerebral Palsy.

Shelley and son Rory moved to sunny Australia 5 years ago and are loving the lifestyle. Shelley continues to enjoy her career as a Speaker, Journalism, Health and Wellbeing, TV, Music and Authoring – happily touching others so that they can be and do their best despite circumstances, whilst having fun and enjoying her journey.

Happiness Guru
at your next
conference

Shelley Sykes known as the '**Happiness Guru**', is a charismatic keynote speaker and human potential expert helping Fortune 500 companies build more effective communications between management, staff and customers for win-win scenarios and healthier, happier environments.

If you wish Shelley to speak, entertain and support your corporation then please contact Shelley directly or ask your preferred speakers bureau to contact Shelley.

Phone: +61 438 016622
Email: shelley@shelleysykes.com

www.shelleysykes.com

About
Edward de Bono

Born in Malta on 19th May, Edward trained as a GP Doctor following in his father's footsteps. Edward has been more enthralled with people, their nature and their way of thinking and communication.

His passion in life is to help people 'think differently' so that they can become more effective learners and leaders of their own lives. He is famous for 'The 6 Thinking Hats' being widely used in schools and universities around the world. His education programs are currently being set up in war torn Sarajevo. His Centre of Thinking in Malta is a meeting place for the governments of the world to bring conflicts to more agreeable settlements.

Happily based in London, he now travels the world as a speaker and consultant.